A Pedagogy of Authority

A Pedagogy of Authority

Marjorie Barrett Logsdon

Learning Moments Press
Pittsburgh, PA

Learning Moments Press
Pittsburgh, PA 15235

www.learningmomentspress.com

Copyright © 2017 by Dorothy Sheehan
All rights reserved, including the right of
reproduction in whole or in part in any form.

ISBN-13: 978-0-9976488-2-9

BISAC Subject:
EDU042000 Education: Essays
EDU040000 Education: Philosophy, Theory & Social Aspects

BISAC Audience:
06 (Professional & Scholarly)

Cover Artwork by Wendy M. Caughey Milne

Book Layout: Mike Murray, pearhouse.com

*To a strong woman—my mother,
Dorothy Barrett Logsdon*

The illustrated cover includes sketches of a cat, sketchbook and crucibles—all of which Marge referred to directly in her writing when describing "The Alchemist," a print displayed in her classroom. Sketching those images for the cover book I struggled to include her words, my style and my relationship to Marge. My initial explorations were filled with large swatches of waxen color with the images collaged throughout in a much more abstract way that didn't seem to capture my impressions of Marge. In my final interpretation I switched to pen and ink sketches but when it came to the frame, I explored my personal memories of Marge in ways that came more easily to me. The abstract swirling lines which tumble from the sketchbook into the frame and then back out of the frame to the bottom of the page are my representation of Marge. Though it's been over 15 years since I sat around a dining room table with Marge I am always reminded of her genuineness and the deep, deep respect she had for her students. How does one represent genuineness and respect? For me, they emerge through a golden color and overlapping swirling, tumbling strands that imply a connection and "going-on-forever." I have to believe, though Marge is no longer with us, the connections she made with her students continue to emerge through them in many powerful ways. In creating this illustration I am reminded of the importance of sharing those strands of Marge with my own students.

Wendy M. Caughey Milne

Contents

FOREWORD   i

Essay One
PRELIMINARY MUSINGS   1

Essay Two
MEMORY TEXTS: INHERITED NOTIONS OF AUTHORITY   21

Essay Three
THE LANYARD AND THE WHISTLE: BEING AN AUTHORITY   43

Essay Four
TURNING TOWARD PORTFOLIOS AND WRITING:
SHARING AUTHORITY   57

Essay Five
THE CRUCIBLE: AUTHORITY AND THE MATTER OF TIME   73

Essay Six
THE CRUCIBLE: AUTHORITY AND THE MATTER OF TEXTS   87

Essay Seven
PEDAGOGY OF AUTHORITY: A MATTER OF MEANING   101

BIBLOGRAPHY   109

FOREWORD

Marjorie Barrett Logsdon, Ph.D. was a friend and colleague, a gifted teacher, an accomplished basketball coach, and a dedicated scholar. She completed her doctoral dissertation 13 years before she died of pancreatic cancer in 2013. Marge left behind a legacy in the students whose lives and minds she touched and in her thoughtful inquiry into the nature of pedagogical authority. *Learning Moments Press* is honored to publish Dr. Logsdon's dissertation, thereby extending her legacy to others who may be struggling to transform their pedagogy.

All too often the rhetoric of teacher reform conveys the impression that improving one's teaching is a matter of mastering new techniques, honing a skill set, or adopting a particular instructional package. Those who work in teacher education know that such changes—while important—merely skim the surface of good teaching. Those who have answered the "call to teach" know that teaching is a relational practice, grounded in one's way of being with students. Inherent in the teacher-student relationship is a power differential and choosing how to use one's power adds a moral and ethical dimension to life in the classroom. In *A Pedagogy of Authority* Marge lays bare her struggle to transform inherited notions of authoritarian power into a shared power to co-author with her students the "text of the classroom."

To portray her struggle, Marge wrote the speculative essays that comprise *A Pedagogy of Authority*. To craft the essays, she drew upon early childhood memories, dreams, experiences as a basketball coach, and experiences as a high school teacher of English literature and composition. The context of teaching composition serves as the crucible for the transformation of Marge's pedagogy. But the implications of Marge's struggle extend beyond the teaching of

English to any teacher who is trying to change the fundamental nature of his or her pedagogical relationship with students.

In the 1980s, three movements began to emerge and converge: teacher reflection, classroom-embedded teacher inquiry, and interpretive modes of inquiry. *A Pedagogy of Authority* has been shaped by all three and thus offers an example for others who might want to engage in a reflective, interpretive inquiry of their practice. In 1991, curriculum scholar William Schubert proposed that speculative essays might serve as a mode of philosophical inquiry.[1] Marge both drew from and extended Schubert's thinking about the essay as a genre, not merely as a representation of *what* one already knows, but as a *way of coming to know* through writing. One might assume that as an English composition teacher Marge easily entered into the writing process, but that would be incorrect. In the first essay, "Preliminary Musings," Marge reveals her struggle to embrace writing as a mode of inquiry. Defying the convention of "never write in the second person," Marge recounts how she "talked herself into the inquiry and the writing." This aspect of *A Pedagogy of Authority* may be reassuring to others who are struggling to enter a process of inquiry.

This book also offers a counterpoint to the simplistic notion that writing is a linear process in which finished texts flow seamlessly from pre-conceived outlines. Fueling the desire to transform her pedagogy was a shift occurring more broadly in the field of English composition—what it means to teach writing as a process rather than as a critique of written products. Inherent in the process approach is the importance of recursive thinking and writing; a concept difficult for Marge's task- and grade-oriented students to accept. Marge, herself, comes to a deeper understanding of what it means to write recursively as she grapples with ideas for her dissertation. Among those of us who accompanied her on the dissertation journey, Marge was notorious for sending out a draft, followed almost immediately with another message, "Ignore what I sent. It's garbage." Of course, any of us would have been more than happy to have written what Marge judged as inadequate. But she was not satisfied until she had shaped her ideas as carefully as possible.

For years, the emphasis in Marge's high school composition classes was the argumentative essay. Students were expected to develop a thesis with supporting evidence. Having been steeped in this writing tradition, Marge confronted two questions. First, in what sense can memories and dreams count as "evidence"? Second, in what sense can writing so personally count as inquiry? Drawing from feminist and psychoanalytic literature, Marge makes the case for mining personal experience as an important source of teacher self-knowledge. While readers might come to different forms of self-knowledge in their own inquiries, Marge's work offers an example of how one can develop a thesis by weaving personal knowledge with theoretic literature. In *A Pedagogy of Authority*, Marge "lets the reader travel the undulating trek of thought and feeling"[2] that she travelled. She concludes the account of her journey with a metaphor of the alchemist whose commitment lies in striving for perfection while recognizing that the process, not the end point, is what really matters.

Maria Piantanida
Publisher

REFERENCES

[1] Willian H. Schubert, "Philosophical Inquiry: The Speculative Essay" in *Forms of Curriculum Inquiry,* ed. E. Short, (Albany, NY: State University of New York Press, 1991).

[2] Schubert, p. 65.

Essay One

Preliminary Musings

MUSINGS ON THE DISSERTATION

The past suggests "that women are well beyond youth when they begin, often unconsciously, to create another story."[1] So it has been with me. Sometime during my thirty year teaching career, I began to compose another story of my "self." I also began to compose another pedagogy. These things happened along the way of authoring a study on a "pedagogy of authority." (You may notice that echoes of Paulo Freire and *Pedagogy of the Oppressed* will sound in several places throughout the study.[2])

What I write in this first speculative essay, "Preliminary Musings on the Inquiry," are the beginnings of that story, reflections on matters of import for this interpretive inquiry. I name the musings: On the Dissertation, Claiming the Study, Coming to the Study, On Writing, On the Speculative Essay, On Authority. In these musings, I trace my initial speculations on features of the inquiry and thus address the need for the author/researcher of a dissertation to write with "a self-conscious method."[3] These sections also show my unfolding awareness that writing doesn't precede thinking; we don't work *from* ideas, we work *toward* them. (One of my former students shared this paraphrase with me. I believe that Bernard Shaw and Borges both said it.) Thus, the "musings" reveal my incipient understandings as an author and researcher who needs "not to translate my subjectivity out of the picture but to take it up with a new sense of responsibility—to make proposals about the world we share with the aim of deepening our collective understanding of it."[4] I end this essay with a brief summary of the successive essays in this text, so that the reader knows what to expect around each bend in the road of my thinking.

MUSINGS ON CLAIMING THE STUDY

You begin a dissertation. The decision comes after attending a dissertation writing group for four years. You are at the "turn-around" age of forty seven—turn around because age begins to bother you—age and seeing an elderly father in and out of hospitals, personal care and skilled care homes. "Managed care" terrifies you in a new way. "*Managed.*" You are in a passage as Gail Sheehy says, but you never did take time to read the book because that type of book was for other women—women who want to think about "life passages," who sort things out, who like Granny Weatherall in the short story by Eudora Welty, make "plans and provisions," women who reflect on themselves and organize their lives. You want to live as it happens without too much painful retrospection, so you often smugly chuckle as you walk past the burgeoning Self-Help section of Barnes and Noble. You *will change*.

The dissertation decision comes after four years in a Ph.D. program, after teaching English in an all-girls' Catholic school for twenty some years, after a State Championship in basketball, after years as yearbook and newspaper advisor, after the "posts"— postmodernism and postfeminism. You finally made the decision after sitting "at the table" for four years—the dissertation study group held every third Thursday in the home of your mentor. But even as you make the decision you realize that it is for others—for those who believe in you, for your mother who so wanted to become a nurse but was needed at home. (If she were alive she would be proud of you, but not say it.) After you realize that the dissertation is for others, you are amused, say "Of course" when you read Heilbrun who notes that Patricia Spacks, in writing about woman and autobiography, talks about a "rhetoric of uncertainty." In "Selves in Hiding," Spacks notices that in the autobiographies of Golda Meir, Eleanor Roosevelt, and Dorothy Day, the theme of accomplishment rarely dominates the narrative, that these women fail in a great degree to emphasize their own importance even though they write in a genre that "implies self-assertion and self-display." They shrink from "claiming that they either sought the responsibilities they ultimately bore or were in any way ambitious."[5]

And so, you begin a dissertation, claiming that you don't *have* to write one for professional purposes or even for yourself. Later, you realize after a "dark night of the soul" as one study group member calls it, that writing for others is not enough, so you make a pact with yourself. Either you will find a way to make this study about authority and your teaching meaningful or you will quit. (The irony in writing a study "for" someone else about your teaching was not lost on you, even as you agonized in the dark night.) After coming to the realization that you do indeed *need* to write, other realizations quickly follow on the heels of the first. You surface fears. You move through nine genealogies of dissertation titles, some because you outgrew them, others because they didn't fit. (Speaking of not fitting you realize that time spent on "The Study" adds six strokes to you golf game and inactivity layers three inches on your waist.)

You "press on" in the oft-quoted words of your mentor, but find dissatisfaction after dissatisfaction with writing. Nothing is good enough for you. Writing the study isn't the way you imagined it. While you declare yourself "fit" to write, the introspection you have always avoided is now not only necessary but an integral part of the process. Neither looking at one's teaching from a distance nor from up close and personal as the saying goes is pleasant. While learning that anguish is often a part of the territory of interpretive inquiry, you keep telling yourself that it's okay to be an ambiguous woman, in the Heilburn sense.[6] But you continually struggle with being a feminist, being a modernist who sometimes thinks like a postmodernist, with being a female teacher writing about a pedagogy of authority.

You think back to the time when the topic of the study was feminist pedagogy. Somehow doubt nagged at you and asked, "Is this what you call what you do in the classroom?" Things just didn't feel right—not the topic, not the writing. So you discarded this topic and placed it on the heap with other "studies" and topics that didn't quite fit. You begin to wonder if anyone writes about the web of self-discovery and self-disclosure or even the pain of self-avoidance in the dissertation process. You wonder if anyone writes about waking up in the middle of the night or not being able to sleep because the dissertation simply refuses to give you up to sleepfulness. Writing an interpretive dissertation from a feminist and literary point of view forces you to acknowledge certain inadequacies.

Then you realize, even as you claim writing as method of inquiry and the "speculative essay"[7] as the genre for the study, that you still hold on to ideas about writing that you learned in the 1960s. But you school yourself and keep trying to move forward, to write with a "sense of trust" that makes discovery possible.[8] Even today you begin (again) to trust. You dream that you are reading a dissertation by a study group member who used second person in a chapter. Why not try this, you think as you dream. Then you awaken and know that she did not use second person in her dissertation. You remember Cate, your student, who wrote using "you" throughout a personal writing. Something caught hold. Why not consider second person, try-on different voices, theorize from another vantage point? You had found something lacking in the narratives you had already written. Perhaps in a paradoxical way, avoiding the first person allows you to "open" the text of the dissertation and will also open another layer of meaning, somehow bring you closer to understanding what you need to express. Perhaps this is what Lopate means when he says that writing the essay "is a mode of inquiry, another way to get at the truth."[9]

You think about Sam Hazo who in *The Pittsburgh That Starts within You* writes an evocative memoir of the city. He says that all memoirs are fragmentary, that the new keeps erasing and transfiguring the old until "you think the past is just something you dreamed." What brought you to this study is similar to what he describes: recollections, fragments, moments settle into memory until each "remembered fragment becomes a puzzle-piece of a long since disassembled puzzle of the city." You liken yourself to Pittsburgh in his memoir and come to see that "each fragment in time's mysterious metamorphosis has already started to evolve into other fragments." You being to realize, as did Hazo, that "changes never end because the city—any city—is not so much a place as it is an idea or rather a gathering of ideas where each idea influences every other idea as it inevitably and ineluctably realizes itself, and the resulting ferment and fusion define what we call a city in the similar differences of every ongoing minute."[10]

And so, after many fits and starts, you finally settle into a retrospective and introspective look at the process of writing a dissertation and writing a teaching life. Like Hazo's portrayal of Pittsburgh, you come to a "gathering of ideas" that landscape the study with memories, dreams, and moments that center on teaching, writing and authority. You write autobiographically about what the "nerves and skin remember."[11] The resulting ferment and fusion continues, like you, to evolve and transform. Even dreams reveal the transformation. In the words of another mentor, you let go of some of the "dysfunctional notions" you held about writing and dissertations. (After all is said and done, nothing about writing from the personal "I" ensures reaching the subjective and nothing about writing from the distanced, the objective, ensures freedom from the subjective and experiential.) You give yourself permission to author, to experiment, to refuse to use" I," to use "I," to dream the use of "you." The voices you give yourself are yours and experimenting with writing practices allows you to see a deeper and more complex relationship with the text and the "self," just as Richardson says.[12] And after many beginnings, you begin to unravel the texts of your teaching, begin to authorize your "self."

Musing on Coming to the Inquiry

Charting the path of coming to the dissertation is not like following a line from point A to B; like writing the path is recursive. At first I wrote narratives of teaching experiences that troubled me, that stuck with me over thirty years of being an English teacher. The stories or memories clustered "like aphids on a rose" as Steinbeck would say, each surfacing some issue around being a woman, teaching, and authority. You may have had this type of remembering, too, where memories refuse to give in to forgetfulness. It's like going to the animal rescue league to select a puppy. You find that the shaggy-haired brown one with one ear slightly higher than the other, with the body of a shepherd and the hair of a poodle, the one that seemed to recognize you as soon as you paused in front of its cage; this is the one you take home. You tell your friends you didn't select the puppy; it picked you. It was like this with my experiences in teaching—certain memories seemed to select me for remembrance, were never far from my conscious recall. In this study I name these memories "memory texts." Literary allusions also surface throughout the writing as part of the memory texts. These allusions, remnants of teaching literature, become a foil for reflection, as Pinar says, and enhance the "conscious and explicit participation in an aesthetic experience."[13]

Initially I wrote narratives of these "memory texts"; wrote with a consciousness of re-telling the stories for an audience. I considered image, word choice and detail, sensory impression—elements a writer selects to re-create a story or memory so that a reader can imagine or understand it. In other words, I carefully crafted the narrative with an eye toward artfulness and effect.

Somewhat paradoxically though, as I continued to write, I remember pushing the idea of an imagined or eventual audience to the background so that I could "release" the story. By this I mean that I laid aside my personal fear of the judgment someone might make and I "bracketed" (as much as possible) my "student" self out of the telling. I "released" both the story and the "self" that worried about how I as the author would "sound," how the story would be judged, and I allowed the most faithful rendering possible to come through. This, I believe, was a significant step in the writing. It was also quite freeing.

It was an odd type of displacement and removal of the authoring self. I was aware that I was writing and aware that I selected particular words or features for these memory texts, yet at the same time I cast myself as a type of Hamlet—a mere agent—called upon to retell the story of the "memory texts." At this point in the study, saying what needed to be said held my ego at bay. As Emig notes of the writing teacher, "the ego of the writing teacher has somehow to stand aside."[14] This is what I did during this phase in my writing—I stepped outside of myself. Just as Hamlet felt called upon by the ghost to exact revenge, I, too, *ironically* felt as if there was something more important than the "self" in the memory texts that needed to come into the light.

After a year passed and I had written what I considered to be the key memories about being a female teacher and authority—these were the DEAD-line story, the Summer Basketball Camp story, and the "Marjorie, Do You Have to Yell" story—I became stuck, paralyzed, and didn't know how to interpret what I had written. It was at this time a mentor suggested Schubert's piece on the speculative essay which I read and then adopted for this study.[15] Instead of staying with my original plan to write an interpretive and literary study with feminist grounding and narrative as the genre, I decided to use the speculative essay as the genre and writing as the method of inquiry. Literary and feminist theory would inform the inquiry.

Initially, I was somewhat intimidated about writing essays, relying only on memory for my thinking about them. (Montaigne, Bacon, Emerson.) Then I reconsidered what Schubert said about the essay and curriculum inquiry. He spoke of John Dewey, Maxine Greene, Madeline Grumet. I thought again. Virginia Woolf, Adrienne Rich, Joan Didion, Barbara Ehrenreich, Anna Quindlen. Acknowledging this heritage, I thought about the personal nature of writing. Then I began to feel more at ease.

Yet, another wave of insecurity hit almost immediately after my naming of names. "Who was I to think that I could write essays?" I asked myself. "Didn't these authors *begin* with something to say?" I was no expert. These thoughts plagued me until I accepted myself as "expert" of my experience. Thirty years of teaching matters, I told myself. And I wanted to write. So, I held troubling notions about these expert essayists in abeyance. Then I read about the essay and read about writing. The more I thought about the speculative essay as blending personal and theoretic writing, the more I thought it suitable for me.

I know I had the personal to draw on—the "matter" of the dissertation, if you will—three decades of experience. Plus two years of teaching journals gave me "texts" for initial reflection. The "speculative" strands would be shaped through writing and literary theory: feminism would also ground the study. And so, after making yet another recursive move, I began to read authors who spoke to my concerns. I found Conway's text, *When Memory Speaks: Exploring the Art of Autobiography*,[16] to be most helpful, and I summarize what she says next.

MUSINGS ON WRITING: THE AUTOBIOGRAPHICAL

Conway notes that in Western Europe and the white settler societies that were its offshoots, life scripts for men and women were archetypal in nature and thus remarkably persistent over time. She traces the "shaping" autobiographical impulse throughout the history of Western thinking (in males) as moving from an odyssey of the external to internal world. In the external world, the hero journeyed through many trials and tests, often physical in nature. Then, under the influence of Christianity, the odyssey prevalent in the classical pattern changed to a story about the inner consciousness of a narrator on a journey of initiation or conversion, poised between sin and damnation or belief or salvation.[17] At the turn of the twentieth century, Conway says, "a new quest for authenticity emerged in

Western European culture,"[18] a modern quest for meaning, given form in classic works like T.S. Eliot's "Ash Wednesday" and "Four Quartets" and James Joyce's *Portrait of the Artist as a Young Man*.

For women, though, the history of autobiographical writing showed "the extent to which experience is both shaped by gendered difference and subject to the same economic and cultural forces which influence the shape and style of male narratives." Conway claims, women inherited a different tradition from classical antiquity than the one that shaped St. Augustine's consciousness. The myth of the adventurous female or hero came through the image of the Amazons, but here the image of the female as powerful is "monstrous rather than admirable." Because women in Greek democracies did not count as citizens, they were left out of political theory and concepts of citizenship. Also, the Pauline influence on the Christian scriptures gave early Christians fear of the senses and the injunction that women should keep silent in church. Thus, Conway notes, the problem of voice for European women was acute, "since their culture defined them as incompetent in or irrelevant to two core areas of speculation about life, politics and theology."[19]

It was in the "special enclave of religious life," notes Conway, that "the tradition of Western European women's autobiography was first established in narratives about the autobiographer's relationship with God."[20] But these writings lacked a "sense of agency and acting on one's own behalf" with which the Greek ideal of the hero is fused. Women like Hildegard of Bingen (12th C) and Dame Julian of Norwich (14th C) and Teresa of Avila (16th C) provide examples which "set the pattern for describing a woman's life in a way that shaped women's subsequent narratives as definitively as the odyssey gave the underlying form to the male autobiography." Thus, the secularization of Europe produced no female Rousseau claiming to be the model of a new social and political type of life. Instead, the secular form of women's narratives "emerged in the bourgeois preoccupation with romantic love, marriage, family and property."[21]

During the nineteenth century, Conway says, the "bourgeois cult of privacy" concerning family and domestic life required women to be silent in their role in family dramas. Thus, because they had to preserve family secrets, women wrote diaries much more frequently than they wrote memoirs. "The mere act of sitting down to write an autobiography broke the code of female respectability because doing so required a woman to believe that her direct experience, rather than her relationships with others, was what gave meaning to her life."[22] This means we should read feminist memoirs as acts of rebellion.

But what of cultural scripting? How did the nineteenth-century woman and the twentieth-century woman convince herself and others that she was the heroine of her narrative? According to Conway, nineteenth and twentieth century women "had great difficulty making themselves subjects and objects of their own stories." Still, by the mid-twentieth century, new and more confident narrative styles were emerging, "although the self-denigrating female narrator seems a permanent part of our culture."[23]

In some women's narratives, "the powerful *I* of the narrator is center stage—in others she is almost a voice speaking from another room, so skillfully is she concealed among the props of the drama."[24] And so, with these ideas in mind, selecting the essay as the genre for this study and claiming my "self" as an author within that center room will enable me to follow in the tradition of Virginia Woolf[25] and declare the *room my own*.

Also, of special interest to me in light of my own writing, is Conway's comment about women authors and their "transitions and shifting narrative styles." She asserts that these elements "are sure signs that their authors are struggling to overcome the cultural taboos that define these women as witnesses rather than actor's in life's events."[26] Experimenting with second person in this essay reveals my struggle to come to agency and shows how experimenting with the text enables me to express my "presence" and "authorial personality" as Harris suggests.[27] In authoring a writing that lays bare the process of coming to understand, I join the "explosion of work about teaching from the perspective of those who teach."[28] While the path I follow is my own, I invite comparison to all who follow similar ways believing that the "current trend of seeking autobiographical narratives of those with extensive experience. . ." will serve as a way of "exploring the basic tenets of a culture."[29]

MUSINGS ON THE SPECULATIVE ESSAY

The essay seemed like a hand-in-glove fit for me both personally and for the public nature of a dissertation with a "pedagogy of authority" as its focus. For one thing, the essay suits the autobiographical character of a study where I use writing as a method of inquiry and discovery. Also, the personal nature of the essay, perhaps its most salient feature,[30] lends itself well to an unfolding of writing and thinking processes. Too, Recchio says that the fundamental ground of the essay is "a critical orientation toward the object of inquiry and towards the subject, that is, the self."[31] Good adds that in essaying, "the writer and the object of inquiry (an experience, an institution, a text, a disciplinary practice, or even one's self as that self is rendered in language) define and transform themselves reciprocally, aspects of each becoming understood in relation to the other."[32] The movement from the personal to the public, writing for myself, writing about myself, and writing to come to understand a "pedagogy of authority" offer a sound blending of method and genre. Writing speculative essays allows me to maneuver in a deliberative and recursive way and reveals to the reader my thinking process as it unfolds.

Since the personal essay is not afraid to reveal its process as it is being written, it "allows the reader to follow the often convoluted journey that leads to greater illumination."[33] This makes the essay suitable for me in terms of personal agency and appropriate for a dissertation with educative value. As Schubert claims, the speculative essay "is a portrayal of the author's way of reflecting" and as such is "a form of philosophical inquiry put into writing."[34] Coming to understand what I am doing as I am doing it—the awareness of myself as a research/writer of the dissertation—making conscious the process of forming the dissertation, is what happens when writing is used as method of coming to know or understand.[35]

Berthoff says of method that it can be simply a procedure or a sequence of activities and in this sense may apply to almost anything from dieting to climbing Mt. Everest. But she claims that method in philosophy is a way of "bringing together what we think we are doing and how we are doing it: *meta + hodos* = about the way; the way about the way."[36] Insisting that English teachers, especially writing teachers, need to become philosophers, Berthoff says that when teachers consider language and thought, theory and practice, and when they think about thinking, they are doing what philosophers do. She takes issue with social scientists who would use the same approach to education as they would to natural sciences. Educational research must be something different from research in natural sciences because education "profoundly and essentially involves language" which she contends is not a natural process but a symbolic form and a social process. Thus, educators should formulate the questions they pursue for consideration as well as the approach they take to inquiry. Berthoff also claims that in a philosophical approach it is better to ask about function instead of essence.[37] In this way, we can focus on how a particular phenomenon—like pedagogy of authority—operates in our life.

As a researcher who assumes a philosophical stance, I also follow Berthoff[38] who encourages us to pronounce research the way that southerners do. *Re'*-search. Thus, re-search she says is a re-flexive act. Educators do not need new data—they do, however, need to reconsider what is already at hand. This is what I do when I provide a thirty year retrospective and introspective study of my teaching experiences. I *spy out, watch or examine*, in the root sense of the word speculate, which comes from *speculari* and also means "to engage in thought or reflection, especially conjectural or theoretical in natures."[39] Thus, as a teacher/researcher I seek, as Coleridge says, to know my own knowledge.[40]

The speculative essay, then, is a genre that is personal, that displays the reflective and the recursive nature of writing. In this aspect, the essay shows its individual and solitary nature. Yet, in its public aspect, the essay is also communal as well as deliberative in nature. For me, a writing/study group of researchers deepened the discursive and deliberative nature of both my writing and thinking for this inquiry and I weave strands of their ideas throughout each essay.

MUSINGS ON AUTHORITY

In many ways, I've spent a lifetime coming to a study about authority, especially teacher authority. While one might think that after thirty years of teaching, I would have resolved my problems with authority, I haven't. While I sense that coming to understand authority will require a change in binary thinking, even now, after settling into the idea of a social construction of knowledge, I realize the residue of either/or thinking still clings to me and I sense a need to move to a more ambiguous place. I sense, too, that coming to understand a pedagogy of authority requires that I move past either/or thinking, to somewhere that Sommers describes as suspended between either *and* or.[41] Evolving ideas keep me on shifting ground. I know and I believe that while there is no way to define a pedagogy of authority, I need to describe some of the things that will help me come to a fuller understanding of it. I sense also that understanding authority, pedagogy, and a pedagogy of authority will continually evolve as I do, as does the context of my teaching, as does each class, each day.

So, it seems appropriate at this point to think about the word authority in its several senses. Edward Said offers a "constellation of linked meanings"[42] about authority including the following definitions based on the *Oxford English Dictionary*: the power to enforce obedience; derived or delegated power; a person whose opinion is accepted and power to inspire belief. There is also a connection between the word authority and *author* that has historical and epistemological import. An author was not only a person who set forth written statements, but a person who originated or gave existence to anything.

There is another cluster of meanings about authority, according to Said that I need to acknowledge. Author is tied to the past participle of *auctus* of the verb *augere*. And *auctor* is literally an increaser and thus a founder. But more than this *auctoritas* is production, invention, cause, the right of possession. "Finally, it means continuance, or a causing to continue," Said adds. Thus, these meanings of authority are all grounded on the following notions:

THAT OF THE POWER OF AN INDIVIDUAL TO INITIATE, INSTITUTE, ESTABLISH—IN SHORT TO BEGIN;

THAT THIS POWER AND ITS PRODUCT ARE AN INCREASE OVER WHAT HAD BEEN THERE PREVIOUSLY;

THAT THE INDIVIDUAL WIELDING THIS POWER CONTROLS ITS ISSUE AND WHAT IS DERIVED THEREFROM;

THAT AUTHORITY MAINTAINS THE CONTINUITY OF ITS COURSE.[43]

These then are some of the sense of the word authority that I explicate in this collection of essays. The first essay, "Preliminary Musings on the Inquiry," represents the starting point of this inquiry. Here I portrayed the pathways I took in claiming authority to "author" this study. In doing this, I talked about the process of authoring and the beginnings of my transformation, a requirement of any hermeneutic work according to Smith.[44] I also laid out the logics for the speculative essay as genre and writing as method of inquiry, emphasizing how this genre bridges personal and theoretic writing and thus blends method and theory. Lastly, I introduced musings on the language I use in the study—authority, method, speculation—and reflected on the meanings these words hold for me.

In the second essay, "Memory Texts: Inherited Notions of Authority," I address this question, "How do I narrate and explicate 'inherited notions' of authority?" Here, I travel back in my past to locate people and experiences that influenced ways I construct authority. Using dreams and other "memory texts," I present a retrospective view of my institutional biography.[45] The essay then allows me to speculate on how experiences and images harbored just within the borders of consciousness become myth-like in affect and influence my taken-for-granted knowledge about authority. I talk, too, about the way past images form "gestalts"[46] that influence me to respond automatically to pedagogical moments. I suggest that these images fulfill a desire for coherence resistant to change and produce an "inherited" authority.

To address the question, "What constructions of knowledge and gender constitute the 'inherited notions'?" I write a third essay called "The Lanyard and the Whistle: Being an Authority" where I look at "the already constituted categories by which we interpret the world."[47] Here I continue to surface experiences from the past, write memory texts about myself as a basketball coach and examine conflicts and contradictions about the gendered nature of "expert" authority. Through the writing of this essay and a feminist perspective, I come to see that "coach" was constructed as male and carried with it assumptions about expert authority. I begin to gain a more complex view of gender that claims identity is neither fixed nor unitary but socially constructed.

In the fourth essay, "Turning toward Portfolios and Writing: Sharing Authority," I describe how I begin to overturn inherited notions of authority by addressing the question: "How do I narrate and explicate a 'pedagogy of authority' that is shifting from teacher-centered to student-centered?" I talk about what I mean by sharing authority with students. I write about my changing pedagogy, setting the story of my life as a teacher of composition (partial and incomplete) against a "biography of the discipline"[48]—also partial and incomplete. I talk about how I move from "thesis" or critical writing to "process writing" that includes narrative forms and portfolio assessment. The process of revising writing with students becomes dialogic and alters my relationship with them. I speculate that the content of the discipline alters the nature of my authority, yet, suggest that painful consequences lie ahead.

The fifth essay, "The Crucible: Authority and the Matter of Time" attends to the question: "What consequences and dilemmas arise from this shifting pedagogy and how do I portray them?" In this writing I use an overarching metaphor of alchemy to talk about the process of altering my consciousness. Here I speculate on authority in a temporal sense, characterize tradition pedagogy as fettered by time, juxtapose it against student-centered approaches, and examine teaching episodes through a concept of "excess."[49] This concept interprets "overflowing semiosis" whereby meaning escapes ideological control and spills into pedagogical practices. Writing this essay helps me see that pedagogical excesses are like the metals of alchemy that must be heated so that they may be tempered. I come to see that if I move to a more expansive consciousness, avoid either/or constructions of authority that place authority either with me or with the students, that I may view pedagogy as *constructing* time rather than *constructed* by it.

In the sixth essay, "The Crucible: Authority and the Matter of Texts," I examine the consequences of shifting to a reader-centered approach to texts. When my new approaches to texts are challenged, I retreat to a traditional role of authority, rely on ritual to convey my pedagogy. Later, I come to realize that my approaches to literature had rested on two opposing constructs of texts: either I opened textual interpretation to any comment, an over-determination of the reader, or I directed textual interpretation to authorized interpretations, an over-determination of text. Using Felman's concept of the implications of psychoanalysis for pedagogy,[50] I interpret my experience and come to realize the way that ignorance and resistance construct knowledge. This helps me understand, much like the medieval alchemist, that things and their opposites may share common elements. I realize, too, that through resistance new understandings may be gained.

The last essay, "Pedagogy of Authority: A Matter of Meaning," attends to the question: "What are the implications of these consequences and dilemmas and how are they constitutive of 'pedagogy of authority'?" A pedagogy of authority uses "author" as an overarching metaphor, but revises historical and literary meanings, overturns notions of fathering and mastering. In this pedagogy I seek to co-author knowledge and authority with students in relationship where each person must take responsibility for meanings that are discursively produced. A pedagogy of authority assumes, as does Freire's pedagogy of the oppressed, that students are active, that they author their own meanings, construct knowledge rather than become passive recipients of the teachers' knowledge.[51] A pedagogy of authority recognizes that "language is not private but shared, and hence meaning is not subjective but intersubjective," that language (and writing) do more than "depict actual states of affairs."[52] So, it is through the process of authoring that I come to authorize myself and a pedagogy of authority.

Notes

1 Carolyn Heilbrun, *Writing a Woman's Life* (New York: Ballantine Books, 1988), 109.
2 Paulo Freire, *Pedagogy of the Oppressed*, trans M.B. Ramos (New York: Herder and Herder, 1970).
3 Brent Kilbourne, "Fictional Theses," *Educational Researcher* (December 1999).
4 David Smith, "Hermeneutic Inquiry: The Hermeneutic Imagination," in *Forms of Curriculum Inquiry*, ed. E. Short (Albany: State University of New York Press, 1991), 201.
5 Heilbrun, *Writing a Woman's Life*, 113.
6 Heilbrun, *Writing a Woman's Life*.
7 William Schubert, "Philosophical Inquiry: The Speculative Essay," in *Forms of Curriculum Inquiry*, ed. E.Short (Albany: State University of New York Press.
8 William Stafford, "A Way of Writing," in *Landmark Essays: On Writing Process* (Davis, CA: Hermagoras Press).

9 Phillip Lopate, *The Art of the Personal Essay: An Anthology from the Classical Era to the Present* (New York: Anchor Books, 1994), xiv.
10 Sam Hazo, *The Pittsburgh that Stays within You* (Pittsburgh, PA: Byblos, 1985) l, 2.
11 Janet Miller, "What's Left in the Field: A Curriculum Memoir" (paper presented at The American Educational Research Association, Montreal, Canada, April 22, 1999).
12 Laurel Richardson, *Fields of Play: Constructing an Academic Life* (New Brunswick, NJ: Rutgers University Press, 1997).
13 William F. Pinar, William M. Reynolds, Patrick Slattery, and Peter M. Taubman, *Understanding Curriculum: An Introduction to the Study of Historical and Contemporary Discourses* (New York: Peter Lang Publishing, Inc. 1995), 415.
14 Janet Emig, "Non-Magical Thinking: Presenting Writing Developmentally in School," in *Essays on Writing, Teaching, Learning, and Thinking*, ed. D. Goswami and M. Butler (Upper Montclair, NJ: Boyton/Cook Publishers, Inc., 1983), 132-133.
15 Schubert, "Philosophical Inquiry."
16 Jill Kerr Conway, *When Memory Speaks: Exploring the Art of Autobiography* (New York: Vintage Books, 1999).
17 Ibid., 7.
18 Ibid., 10.
19 Ibid., 11.
20 Ibid.
21 Ibid., 13.
22 Ibid, 85-86.
23 Ibid., 88.
24 Ibid.
25 Virginia Woolf, *A Room of One's Own* (Orlando, FL: Harcourt Brace Jovanovich, 1957/1929).
26 Conway, *When Memory Speaks*, 88.
27 Wendell Harris, "Reflections on the Peculiar Status of the Personal Essay," *College English*, 58, no. 8 (1996).
28 Sari Knopp Bilken, "Foreword," in *Beginning in Retrospect: Writing and Reading a Teacher's Life*, ed. P. Schmidt (New York: Teachers College Press, 1997).
29 Rita S. Brause, "Foreword," in *Teaching College English and English Education: Reflective Stories*, ed. T.H. McCracken, R.L. Larson, and W.J. Entes (Urbana, IL: National Council of Teachers of English, 1998), ix.
30 Each of the following authors addresses the personal aspect of the essay: Harris, "Reflections on the Peculiar Status of the Personal Essay," Schubert, "Philosophical Inquiry: The Speculative Essay," Lopate, *The Art of the Personal Essay*. Full references for these citations can be found in chapter two notes.

31 Thomas Recchio, "On the Critical Necessity of 'Essaying'," in *Taking Stock: The Writing Process Movement in the 90's*, ed. L. Tobin and T. Newkirk (Portsouth, NH: Boynton/Cook Publishers, 1994), 219.
32 Good quoted in Recchio, "On the Critical Necessity of 'Essaying,'" 219-220.
33 Schubert, "Philosophical Inquiry," 69.
34 Ibid., 66.
35 This view of writing is advocated by Emig, "Non-Magical Thinking: Presenting Writing Developmentally in School" (see note 14); Sandra Perl, "Understanding Composing," in *Landmark Essays of Writing Process*," ed. S. Perl (Davis, CA: Hermagoras, 1980/1994); Laurel Richardson, "Writing: A Method of Inquiry," in *Handbook of Qualitative Research*, ed. N.K. Denzin and Y.S. Lincoln (Thousand Oaks, CA: Sage, 1994).
36 Ann E. Berthoff, *The Making of Meaning: Metaphors, Models and Maxims for Writing Teachers* (Upper Montclair, NJ: Boynton/Cook Publishers, Inc., 1981), 4.
37 Ibid., 28.
38 Berthoff, *The Making of Meaning*.
39 *The Compact Edition of the Oxford English Dictionary* (Oxford, London: Oxford University Press, 1971), 557.
40 Coleridge quoted in Berthoff, *The Making of Meaning*, vi.
41 Nancy Sommers, "Between the Drafts," in *Women/Writing/Teaching*, ed. J.Z. Schmidt (Albany: State University of New York Press, 1998), 61
42 Edward Said, *Beginnings: Intention and Method* (New York: Basic Books, 1975).
43 Ibid., 83.
44 Smith, "Hermeneutic Inquiry," 198.
45 Deborah Britzman, *Practice Makes Practice: A Critical Study of Learning to Teach* (Albany: State University of New York Press, 1991).
46 Fred A. Korthagen and Joseph Kessels, "Linking Theory and Practice: Changing the Pedagogy of Teacher Education," *Educational Researcher* (May 1999).
47 Maxine Green, The Lived World," in *The Education Feminist Reader*, ed. L. Stone (New York: Routledge, 1994), 113.
48 Kathleen M. Ceroni, e-mail to author, July 2000.
49 John Fiske, *Understanding Popular Culture* (London: Routledge, 1991).
50 Shoshana Felman, "Psychoanalysis and Education: Teaching the Terminable and Interminable," *Yale French Studies* no 63 (June 7, 1982).
51 Freire, *Pedagogy of the Oppressed*.
52 Thomas Schwandt, "On Understanding Understanding," Qualitative Inquiry 5, no. 4 (1999): 453.

Essay Two

Memory Texts: Inherited Notions of Authority

MEMORY AND INSTITUTIONAL BIOGRAPHY

We each carry with us what Britzman names an "institutional biography."[1] "Unlike autobiography, which is very idiomatic, institutional biographies are made from defined roles and functions (such as teacher or student), have routines that occur regardless of the person, and offer definitional guides or coersions (measures of right and wrong that preclude situation and context) that one must confront or live." Thus, she says, the story of a student, "is also the story of an institution. Same with the teacher's story: the story of the institution."[2]

Our institutional biographies then are repositories of our experiences and contain some "well-worn and commonsensical images of teacher's work."[3] We recall with relative ease images of a teacher, located behind a desk or in front of the chalkboard, a teacher feared or disliked, cherished or admired. Even when the reach of memory must travel backward through decades, remembering teachers and classrooms, picturing the way we clustered for reading as blue birds, red birds, or robins—these images remain with us and form texts that comprise our institutional biography. It is this collection of images and experiences that accounts for the "persistency of particular world views, orientations, dispositions, and cultural myths that dominate our thinking and, in unintended ways select the practices that are available to educational life."[4]

I explore several educational texts here, speculate how experiences and images harbored just within the borders of memory effect a type of thinking and a knowledge I call inherited. Pursuing these images into language, chasing them from hiding so to speak, is how I begin. The images and experiences hold importance for me because they operate, as Clark notes, as "implicit theories" that guide practice.[5] Sometimes these images repose in a library of teaching experiences that I now recall because they *invite* recall. Composing narratives that I call "memory texts" is how I transform images and events into language, how I begin a process of introspection, a reflective journey undertaken to rediscover the paths I've traveled.

In recording memory texts, I begin with the assumption that "We only store in memory things of value."[6] We remember things that have significance in some way or that are problematic or unfamiliar and in need of review.[7] Brunner posits that "what does not get structured narratively suffers loss in memory."[8] Accepting these views, I begin with a retrospective of images and remembrances so that memory and writing may give shape to the past so that through reflection I may come to understanding. Once memory and writing shape narrative, I then follow Haug's theory of memory-work.[9] The task of memory work, as Crawford aptly puts it "is to uncover and lay bare earlier understandings in the light of current understandings, thus elucidating processes of construction involved."[10] I focus on memories and events about authority, particularly authority as it is embodied in teacher and parent figures. I write, in other words, to come to know what it is I know.[11] I write to come to understand what knowledges of authority I have "inherited." In gathering images into narrative, I wish to discover, as Polanyi suggests, how images represent tacit knowledge.[12] In seeking to reclaim my educational biography, I also seek to "reclaim my imagination," a process Berthoff says may be gained through writing.[13]

INHERITED IMAGES

Father Stokely pronounced it "the finest parish in the world." St. Mary. An old time parishioner recalled for me this "priest-builder" who in 1950 saw the "blueprint for the new high school carried into steel and stone" almost a quarter of a century after he turned the earth over for the construction of the church.[14] She told the story about how Father Stokely would turn from mass, stop abruptly, and then tell late comers to take a seat; told me with the same type of fondness and hand-on-your-arm insistence that my mother used when she told the story about how her father "threw the crate of strawberries over the hill" in a fury at the huckster. Father Stokely liked to pride himself on the church manners of St. Mary's parishioners—"the finest in the world." My mother liked to remember my grandfather Barrett, her Irish Catholic father, and the day "it rained strawberries."

My mother and the elderly parishioner spoke of these fathers with pride. The way the women held on to these images and told their stories tells me something worth keeping lay behind the telling. I remember their admiration. It seemed that they, like the neighbor in Frost's "Mending Wall," would not "go behind their father's saying" and so each woman gave her story to me. Now I recount those stories here. Yet, I'm left to wonder if the cushion of years softened the memory for these women, made acceptable the public performance of irritation and anger in the pastor and my grandfather. But then, perhaps there was nothing to soften. Acting from the pulpit as pastor or from the person of father entitled these men to their anger. Parishioners, after all, should be on time, and hucksters should not bring Irish policemen to temper. Still, I wonder now what impulse or necessity in me called these stories forth for re-telling.

I do know that their stories will not quit me nor I them. I own these memories now just as surely as each story became a part of the St. Mary and Barrett mythology. Years after I had graduated from St. Mary, in fact ten years after the diocese closed it to form a merger with another all-girls' Catholic school, Fr. Stokely came to mind again in the words of a school counselor. "I always wanted to be a St. Mary's girl," she had told me. Her admission threw me back to the image of a man I had never seen and reminded me of the parish and school that he called "the finest in the diocese."

I think now about the images we store; the memories we house; the memories we reproduce. I think about the way we cling to beliefs, make myths from our stories. Inheriting memories of my grandfather and Father Stokely caused me to construct images of my mother's father and images of this "priest-builder" and his apparent pride of place, a pride passed down to me when I became a St. Mary's student. The legacy of Fr. Stokely I inherited from my teachers and then from the elderly parishioner shaped the teacher I became. The image of a priest unseen, this priest I reconstructed in my memory, became fixed in my mind's eye on his pulpit just as if I had seen him there, his words reverberating in my memory even though I never heard him speak. His command to the latecomers to church to take a seat became an image of authority. That image resides in my memory, waiting review and reflection. Too, I rarely heard Grandfather Barrett speak, and knew him only as a gentle man, but I imagine him hurling that basket of strawberries over the hill. Now, even as I write this, I am reminded that "Every psyche is a private theater filled with scenes and characters" where those places and people "still inhabit you."[15] Even people we've never met.

EXCELLENT WOMEN

Sr. Maria Mercuri remains a part of the landscape that I construct of my student days at St. Mary. Even after thirty years, her voice and image stay with me as I recall her oft repeated refrain: "Her voice was ever so soft, Gentle, and low, an excellent thing in a woman."[16] This quote from King Lear came to symbolize Sister and her authority; served, too, as an ideal I was to follow as a student; the ideal that I later imitated as a teacher.

Even now I picture Sr. Mercuri holding her index finger in the air as she precisely pronounced each word in the line; her lips drawn thin and tight with a restraint clearly evident. I see images of her as she stopped girls in the hall, lifting the finger and repeating "soft, Gentle and low" as if these words expressed all one needed to know about the ways to act or to be in the world if one were a female. Sister impressed her will and asserted her authority without ever raising her voice. Always gentle, always soft-spoken, always in control, like Cordelia, she modeled a restraint and authority that bespoke femininity, commanded respect not only because of the flowing black habit of her order, but also because of a powerful personal presence. As a student I clearly remember feeling that failure to model her behavior would bring the type of response that Lear heaped on Cordelia—banishment, a fall from grace, loss of privilege. And *shame*.

The emotional residue that clings to my image of Sr. Mercuri shows how images carry affect, which Bartlett claims is the basis of all perceiving and remembering.[17] Not only are images infused with emotional involvement, they also synthesize perception and experience according to Langer.[18] This is why I connect the failure to obey Sister or to speak in a soft, gentle and low voice with shame. When I re-create the image through writing, I begin to see how the image forms the core of my memory, so that I may begin to understand how the image is central to my notions of authority.

Patricia Hampl in explaining her approach to memoir says:

. . .I EXPLORED THE MYSTERIOUS RELATIONSHIP BETWEEN ALL THE IMAGES I COULD ROUND UP AND EVEN MORE IMPACTED FEELINGS THAT CAUSED ME TO STORE THE IMAGES SAFELY AWAY IN MEMORY. STALKING THE RELATIONSHIP, SEEKING THE CONGRUENCE BETWEEN THE STORED IMAGE AND HIDDEN EMOTION—THAT'S THE REAL JOB OF MEMOIR.[19]

The hidden emotion is what makes the image powerful, and it is also what leads me to re-enact in the present what I "see" from my past.

The significance then of my memories of Sr. Mercuri, Fr. Stokely, and Grandfather Barrett is how their images comprise my educational biography and shape my teacher subjectivity. I call these images forth now because "Over time, the value (the feeling) and the stored memory (the image) may become estranged."[20] It is through writing images into narrative that I "ready" the image and make it available for reflection. It is through writing that I seek to re-unite the image with the emotion so that I may come to know how image maintains the pull on me. It is through writing that image as visual representation meets language as symbolic representation. As poet Heather McHugh says, "I don't write to say what I mean, I write to see what I mean."[21] In uncovering image and connecting it to language, I see how tacit knowing illuminates cultural knowing. Writing images then becomes a way to "focus on the self in social context."[22] A "re-evoked image," Fleckenstein asserts, "contains traces of the initiating perceptions and the influence of culture."[23]

For me, the images held in memory need to be recovered and surfaced through writing so that narrative may "bring [my] thoughts to a more developed stage of utterance."[24] For me, writing images into language is a way to dialogue with the imagination, the most speculative instrument we have according to Berthoff. And imagination can help us with the concept of forming, which Berthoff says depends on abstraction, symbolization, selection, purposing and giving shape to content. "Forming is mind in action," she says; "[i]t is what we do when we learn, when we discover or recognize, when we interpret; when we come to know. Forming is how we make meaning."[25]

The significance of memory, these images I surface for remembrance, reminds me of a question put to Robert Frost. While giving a poetry reading to a group of students, the poet was asked what determined a good poem. "If it lasts," Frost replied. Something similar might be said of memory—significant ones last, show remarkable resistance to forgetfulness. Perhaps Kermode offers a keener insight: "Memory invents a past to defend us against the appalling timelessness of the unconscious."[26]

PEDAGOGY AND SNEAK ATTACKS

"Good combination of sneak attacks and calling on volunteers," my principal commented on the evaluation form, pleased with this aspect of my teaching. I read the comment but recall taking no pleasure in it. Something in her wording interrupted my breathing, gave me a moment's pause. The feeling was palpable; it lingered for a while as I read her other comments; but I then put it out of mind. Leaving the feeling unnamed somehow kept me safe; avoidance, after all, is insulating. If naming is an act of power, as Rich says, it is also a way to come to know.[27] But some knowledge is terrible in its intimacy, as if it knows us before we know it. This is why the act of naming may also bring fear, a fear of knowing.

In the late 1980s when my principal made this comment, I wasn't yet ready to name my knowledge, so I avoided the confrontation of naming and continued a pedagogy of "sneak attacks." I called on the student who *didn't* raise her hand, whose eyes avoided mine. I knew this tactic kept students off-balance and somewhat tense. Wary, alert, on-guard—students had to continually watch for me, anticipate the swiftness and randomness of my actions.

Even today, after consciously trying to remake myself as a teacher, I sometimes find myself reverting to "sneak attacks." When an honors student is "not being faithful" to her reading, or if my temper flares because a student lacks attentiveness during a discussion, I take the offensive, launch into a sneak attack. In performing a pedagogy that I now not only question, but reject, I'm left to wonder about the recalcitrant nature of my behavior. How is it that I continue to enact a practice even after I have come to reject it? In what ways does the past intrude on the present, calling on "inherited" knowledge, eliciting behaviors I no longer consider appropriate? In what ways do images from the past comprise teaching practices in the present?

IMAGES, GESTALTS, MYTHS AND AUTHORITY

I believe, as does Johnston, that images "are more than passive visual recordings of past experiences."[28] For me, they are a sensual remembrance held in the imagination. When summoned for reflection and put into language, images bring understanding to memory. Fr. Stokely and Sr. Mercuri remain etched in memory because they represent images of *being in authority* that I carry with me; images that have become "internalized in such a way. . .[they become] part of the natural order of things."[29] The continuing presence of these images commands my attention and obedience just as Father commanded the obedience of parishioners and Sister commanded obedience of students. In recalling these images, I reach "into the past, gathering up experiential threads meaningfully connected to the present" as Connelly and Clendenin describe."[30]

Another way to interpret the intractable nature of my sneak attacks is to say they arise from a type of knowledge embedded in what Korthagen and Kessels call gestalts. A gestalt is a formation, often "unconsciously or semi-consciously" shaped, that helps us see objects or situations as an entity and causes us to respond to them automatically. According to this theory, complex cultural, psychological, or social knowledge may be embedded in a particular situation, but a gestalt gathers these complexities into one perceptual identity. Korthagen and Kessels say gestalts are activated when teachers make "split second" decisions. These authors would say that in repeating sneak attacks I draw on a gestalt because it contains a "unity of perception, interpretation, and action."[31] When I draw on sneak attacks, even after I have come to reject the pedagogical practice they represent, I unconsciously draw on images of teachers being *in authority*.

I now see that my sneak attacks demand compliance from students in the way that I imagined Fr. Stokely commanded tardy parishioners to be seated or in the way that Sr. Mercuri commanded me to be compliant. The images of the priest and the sister remain ingrained in memory, cause me to take their authority for granted, not only because of the role denoted by their religious vestments, but because in assuming their role they moved beyond the individual to portray the universal, the mythic.

Campbell claims that our response to a judge would be different if the judge wore a suit and not the traditional robe.[32] This, no doubt, offers one way role becomes identifiable and notions of authority constructed. If we accept Campbell's idea, then the robe of a judge helps to carry the meaning of the role, in the same way that the robes of Fr. Stokely and Sr. Mercuri carried meanings about priests and teachers. Through the role, each person then becomes enjoined with a collective. But more than this, because of the symbolic and the collective, the roles may also represent the mythic. Garman tells us that myths are not always examined as are other forms of knowledge.[33] "That we are unconscious of most of our cultural knowledge," Bowers writes, ". . . accounts for our being unaware of the authority culture has over us."[34] Britzman says that the comment, "Funny, you don't look like a teacher" also underscores the power of the image and the power of the mythic, showing how "the multiple identities of teachers get lost in a cycle of cultural determinism."[35]

When my students fail to listen to me or have "not been faithful to their reading," I slip into sneak attacks because the students mirror behaviors that I associate with challenges to being in authority. In other words, a student is not merely challenging me; she is challenging the collective, what I represent through the mythic ideal of "teacher." So, in an ironic sort of way, I respond as an individual for the ideal attached to the many. I carry, as teacher in authority, the burden of my position, the responsibility to uphold the values embedded in the cultural role of teacher. The weight of this responsibility, the awareness of being an individual and at the same time representing the cultural is, I believe, part of the tension and exhaustion teachers feel from the daily enactment of the role. Wearing the mantle of teacher, the robe of authority, is wearing a weighty role indeed. If we ask, as did Waller, what teaching does to teachers,[36] we might ask, too, how the role itself is worn by teachers, inscribed within them, marked on them, and felt, often in unconscious ways.

Thus, we need to call forth images from our past, images that like the "outcroppings granite" of Wharton's New England,[37] remain in the crevasses of memory unexamined, never reaching conscious recall. We need to do this because images "form the subconscious assumptions on which practice is based."[38] I repeat "sneak attacks" even after I recognize and acknowledge them as contrary to new teaching beliefs. In doing this, I replicate behaviors that I as a student may have experienced as harmful or hurtful. Just as in cases of abuse where the abused becomes the abuser, I reproduced behaviors that have caused me pain or anguish. In replicating these behaviors as a teacher, my teaching behaviors became naturalized, and I enact a role formed in the images of a collective.

The knowledge that underlies behavior, tacit and often unexamined, is insidious and powerful. I believe we need to reconstruct our institutional biographies, not just from events, but from the distant and inherited stories and images. We need to take a journey inward, find the images or specters of the past whose present presence in our teaching practice are visible and manifest. Taking an inward journey is fraught with difficulty and risk, but the greater risk is not to "know our own knowledge."[39] With this in mind, I turn to another memory text, teacher dreams, dreams that "haunt" me and contain more than the purely "idiomatic" as Britzman notes.[40] I believe that Felman's theory of the unconscious would extend to dreams because they offer "a knowledge which is not authoritative, which is not that of a master, a knowledge that does not know what it knows."[41] But dreams may teach me something, as they did Freud; they may offer a learning, a text for interpretation.

INTRODUCTION—DREAMS

Virginia Woolf claims that "it is in our idleness, in our dreams, that the submerged truth comes to the top."[42] Transforming dream into narrative then may open other aspects of my educational biography for interpretation. Dreams, the shadow side of consciousness as

Doll frames them, are representations of the same type of image that we cling to in other memories, and they "may enable all of us to confront what shades our perceptions."[43] Teacher dreams then may offer images of the unconscious teacher self, images that form what Felman calls "unmeant knowledge."[44] If, as Finke contends, a person forms subjectude through discursive processes, and is not always fully conscious or present to those processes or the unconscious, "then we need to rethink the very notion that what is significant about teaching is available for conscious and rational analysis." Extending these ideas then, it becomes important to realize that pedagogy, too, "must be characterized by some form of intervention in the unconscious."[45]

I believe that dreams, as memory texts, are images in search of completion in the same way that gestalts aim for closure.[46] Dreams then may comprise gestalts also. In this sense, it becomes the task of the dreamer as Doll says, not to figure images out, but to *figure them in*; "to see, in other words, the figure each image makes."[47] For Doll, an analysis of image patterns in dreams is one way for teachers to face fears that are hidden in another text—the fictional.[48] McMahon adds that the fictional may provide a "form to portray my lived experiences" in a way that encourages me "to respect the complexities and ambiguities with which I am confronted in my practice." If I extend what McMahon says about fiction to dreams, they are then a type of fictional text or "fictional representation of reality," which will enable me "to gain a different view of myself," the unconscious self, so that I may reflect on my teaching from a different perspective, so that "I am less likely to take what it is I know. . . for granted."[49]

TEACHER DREAMS I

Cindy tells me that the previous night she awoke from a dream, "in a cold sweat." In this dream, our newly appointed president was evaluating Cindy's English class, but she could not quiet her sophomores. She tells me that an intense sense of apprehension and anxiety awakened her. We've talked about teacher dreams before, but she remarks that this one was unusual both for its intensity and that she dreamed it right before Christmas vacation. We've talked previously about how teacher dreams usually occur in September at the beginning of the school year.

I say that I've had similar dreams about our new president. In one dream I am in line during an academic procession for graduation and feel the president watching me. I fail to correct a senior who is talking. I begin to feel remiss and I am also keenly aware of the president. I tell my dream to Cindy and jokingly say, "We must both be paranoid." We know the president doesn't make classroom observations. Besides, Cindy is the most loved and respected teacher on our faculty. A few weeks before her dream, the students had named her "Teacher of the Month." For her to dream about being watched, losing control of the students, and to express some form of anxiety, really seems out of the realm of possibility.

Through this encounter and my own experiences, I am drawn to consider teacher dreams, these "fictional representations of reality." I seek to retrieve them to uncover the images and emotions that form them. Like my other memory texts, teacher dreams will not quit me for they have re-occurring themes and plot lines. I need to think about what they hold for me, examine why I can't release them into forgetfulness. Even as I begin to reflect on these dreams, I feel an affinity with Hamlet: I could be "bounded in a nutshell" and count myself "[queen]of "infinite space," but for "bad dreams."[50]

TEACHER DREAMS II

I wrote the following in my teaching journal on November 10, 1997.

It happens again. School dreams. I have several in one night. In the first dream, I am in the high school where I now teach, but the school is out of place, located in Hazelwood where I grew up instead of the East End. The "dream" school is over the railroad tracks, beyond St. Mark's school and church. It begins with me in my classroom.

I stand in a square room with rows of desks and students surrounding me on three sides. I remember telling students to be quiet and one, Jessie, catches my eye. She is the only student I recognize. I repeatedly tell students to get quiet and they simply won't. I stand in the center of the desks that surround me and issue ultimatums. "This is what will happen to you if you don't. . ." Ultimatums. I remember sort of yelling or at the very least raising my voice. I start to talk about texts and hear myself say, "If you don't bring your books to class, I will. . ." I don't remember finishing the statement. Then I issue another ultimatum. "If you fail to. . ." and I can't recollect what else I say.

I make each declaration emphatically and feel myself getting quite angry, but no one in the room cares about what I have to say. Students look at me blankly, as if my presence and my commands don't interest them in the least. They treat me the way they treat Marcy, a teacher in another school, who students laugh at and disrespect.

During the dream—or in that in-between state when we are not soundly asleep and yet not fully awake—I remember thinking: "This is horrible. I can't stand this; I don't want to go down this road again." I connect this dream with my changing pedagogy. Students now treat me the way they treat Marcy.

Then I remember another dream from the night. I was in my present classroom and one student after another comes to me to ask if she can take a make-up test. I'm trying to grade scene enactments while this is going on. Then several students walk into the room dressed for their scene enactments. They look as if they will enact a wedding. I see a bride and several students are singing. I remember turning to a student sitting next to me. She is quite tall, and is an adult, not a high school student. "Do you need to take the exam, too?" I ask her. As she says, "Yes," I realize that she is Betty Jean, a former classmate of mine from high school. I haven't seen her in twenty years.

Then the most tense part of the dream occurs. I reach for my literature text and begin to flip through the pages, searching for the page numbers to give to students who need to make-up an exam. I keep turning pages and can't locate the place I need and feel myself getting more and more frustrated. The students who are performing the scene enactments continue to play their parts, and the other students wait for me to give them the assignment. I feel rushed and realize that there is not much time left in the class. Suddenly, the scene shifts. I find myself walking up Elizabeth Street, past St. Mark's School.

I've left my room and keep walking and walking. I begin to think that I should get back to the class before the bell rings so the students won't just dismiss themselves and leave. I turn to walk back to my room and from outside I hear the bell ring. I hurry as fast as I can. I walk faster and faster, hurrying and hurrying. I arrive at the bridge that crosses the tracks and turn up the hill toward St. Mark's School. Then I awaken.

TEACHER DREAMS III

In this dream I am in front of students in a long rectangular room with no chalkboards. The room is covered in ceramic tile, like one would find in a locker room or swimming pool. It reminds me of Brown Elementary, where I attended kindergarten. I remember seeing that the students were standing in orderly rows.

I ask the students to "Quiet Down," but they ignore me. No one even looks at me when I speak. Again I say," Girls, sit down and be quiet." Still I am ignored. I feel myself getting more and more angry. I finally reach a point of desperation and yell, "If you don't sit down, I will lower everyone's grade one letter grade for this quarter." Still, I get no response from the students. They continue to talk as if I am not there.

Although I can't get them to sit down I somehow manage to get several students out of the room. I usher them into the hall, thinking

I suppose that if I isolate a few I will be able to get better control. I send these students somewhere and I see them as they pass by me as I hold the door open. Anne passes by me and she is the only student I recognize. I then lead one girl to a chair in the hall with a very high wooden back. It is the type of chair with scrolls and deep mahogany wood, the type a bishop would use for a church service. I tell the student to sit in the chair and begin to vent my wrath on her, push my finger into her arm, and feel the flesh give under my index finger. She is tall—5'8" and large framed; I notice this even when she is seated. "You are really out of line," I say. Yet she is unmoved.

We are in a long tunnel-like a place and not a school hall. It resembles the tunnel that passed under the building at St. Mary that we used when it rained. As I am talking to this student, several other students pass by us. I continue to talk to this girl and inform her about her behavior as other students continue to file past. I know I should go back because the bell is about to ring. I worry that something may have happened while I was out of the room and I feel pressured to hurry back to make sure nothing went wrong.

The scene shifts again and I find myself walking back toward the room, but I am still quite angry, and I don't want to go back. I feel an intense anger and say to myself, "I don't like them." I feel caught. Everything I feel says "don't go back" and yet duty or obligation compels me forward. I remember the tunnel I am walking through is moist and damp. The floors are concrete, smooth and painted deep red, just like the tunnel at St. Mary, but I am in the high school where I teach. I make it back to the room just as the bell rings and the students are leaving. They do not speak to me and I do not speak to them. The dream ends.

THINKING THROUGH DREAMS

I'm struck by the intensity of the emotion I felt when I had these dreams and by the contrasting emotional flatness of the dream narratives as I write them here. Perhaps when I dream the visual imagery is so powerful, so intimately connected to personal feelings, that the visual loses its impact when I render the dream into language. Too, in the dream-narratives that I re-construct here, I offer no reason or explanation for the student behavior and only write a simple straightforward plot line of what I remember. But I suspect that as the dreamer I feel an emotional intensity not captured in the dream narrative because while I am dreaming *I am aware of and feel the depth of my anxiety*. It is an anxiety or fear hidden in the "shadow," the dream, hidden also behind the role I enact as teacher. The role cloaks my fear, hides my anxiety. While I dream, my awareness of this unconscious knowledge is what surfaces. It is what I feel when the "I" who is the dreamer (and teacher) observes the "I" who is teacher in the dream. I bear witness to the teacher in the dream who is failing at being in authority. My dream then becomes a dream of recognition where I confront "fears hidden" in a fictional dream text.

My fears, of course, are rooted in a fear of failure—the failure of authority. This is where the dream content represents fears that remain unnamed in my daily teaching life. Thompkins talks about teacher dreams and claims that, in one form or another, the type of dream that I have is "dreamed by thousands of teachers before the beginning of the fall semester." Teacher dreams are remarkably similar in nature she claims. Some teachers dream they can't find their classroom and that they are racing frantically through darkened halls. Others dream they are pontificating in nasal tones about subjects they know nothing about. Still others, Thompkins says, see themselves turning to write on the chalkboard and feel the students leaving behind their backs. The dream is so common she says that many people "discount it."[51]

But the dreams should not be discounted. Thompkins believes the dreams represent an "internalized" fear carried in our teacher images from the past. The image of the "stern teacher" who "stands in front, who stands when others sit, the one whom you must obey, who exacts obedience." This is the teacher that tends to remain in most people's memories. Thompkins relates stories from her past about students who were publicly chastised by teachers: "the quiet innocent, made to stand by his desk in third grade"; the "terror boy" in second grade, who "wouldn't be quieted." She talks about, "The admirable rough and tumble boy who wouldn't sit, wouldn't cooperate, who constantly caught the metaphorical whip and who made the teacher so angry that it spilled onto every class member who witnesses the frequent loss of temper and public disciplining." These teacher images are what we store in memory and what we duplicate as teachers. These are the images, according to Thompkins, that carry with them notions of authority and the knowledge that "Unless I perform for the authorities, unless I do what I am told, I will be publicly shamed."[52] These are the images that we come to mirror and reflect when we perform the role of teacher. And it is the fear or shame of losing one's authority that surfaces in teacher dreams because, as Thompkins asserts, authority "points to the heart of what it means to be a teacher."[53]

These images of teachers gain power over us even when the image moves out of the realm of the actual and into the realm of the dream. In dreams, the fictional texts of the unconscious, these images lodge as "shadows" of us, and like shadows they may prove illusive and difficult to define. In talking about dreams, Doll claims that they offer us "archetypal images that have been safely caged too long."[54] She means that we need to make these images available for educational reflection so that we may come to a fuller understanding of our practice. The image in the dreams then, archetypal in nature, helps to form images of teachers that become models we unconsciously seek to imitate. These images then become myth-like in affect and play out in ways teachers enact their roles.

Britzman also talks about the way myths operate in the lives of teachers. She says that "mythic images" of teachers tend to "sustain and cloak the very structure which produces them." She claims that while the structure of teaching is characterized by isolation, "it is also sustained by the value placed on individual effort."[55] In this valorization of the teacher as the only actor, as autonomous, the teacher takes on "mythic proportions."[56] Another myth according the Britzman is that teachers make themselves. This tends to make teachers de-emphasize theory, and "infuses the individual with undue power and undue culpability." Thus, when a teacher is individualized, or when teachers believe that they make themselves, the social context of teaching dissolves and pedagogy "becomes a product of one's personality."[57] If this is so, then failure, too, becomes individualized and a product of one's personality.

SPECULATIONS ON AUTHORITY

Through reclaiming images and dreams from the past that comprise my "institutional biography,"[58] I re-construct portraits of people in authority that I have *internalized* and *idealized*. These portraits, myth-like in affect, form "a conception of how things are supposed to be, to work, or behave."[59] But more than this, the images or portraits come to represent what I have known and what is familiar to me, blending an idealized "other" with "self," past experience with present pedagogy, giving me a *unified* concept of the *kind of person I am supposed to be* and forming notions of how I, as a teacher, am supposed to relate to the world.[60]

In a significant way, the images that comprise my institutional biography give an illusion of continuity to my experience and fulfill a *desire for coherence* that I then enact as a teacher who is "in authority." As the images from memory texts play behind me on a kind of scrim curtain, I perform a pedagogy on the stage of the present that is shaped by those images. The images are unchanging and offer a kind of reassurance within the uncertain and contradictory context of the classroom and the "self." The teacher "self" I then construct is singular, unified, and non-contradictory; a teacher who satisfies her need for coherence through inherited images, who speaks in a voice of acquired authority,[61] who enacts *a pedagogy primarily authored by inherited knowledge and images from the past*.

NOTES

1 Deborah Britzman, *Practice Makes Practice: A Critical Study of Learning to Teach* (Albany: State University of New York Press, 1001), 3.
2 Deborah Britzman, e-mail to author, June 2000.
3 Deborah Britzman, *Practice Makes Practice*, 3.
4 Ibid.
5 Christopher M. Clark, "Asking the Right Questions about Teacher Preparation: Contributions of Research on Teacher Thinking," *Educational Researcher* 29, no.2 (1988).
6 Patricia Hampl, "Memory and Imagination," in *The Dolphin Reader*, ed. D. Hunt (Boston: Houghton Mifflin Company, 1986), 701.
7 Frigga Haug, *Female Sexualization: A Collective Memory*, trans. E. Carter (London: Verson, 1987).
8 Jerome Bruner, *Acts of Meaning* (Cambridge, MA: Harvard University Press, 1990), 56.
9 Haug, *Female Sexualization*.
10 Jane Crawford, Susan Kippax, Jenny Onyx, Una Gault, and Pam Benton, *Emotion and Gender: Constructing Meaning from Memory* (London: Safe, 1992), 40.
11 Ann E. Berthoff, *The Making of Meaning: Metaphors, Models and Maxims for Writing Teachers* (Upper Montclair, NJ: Boynton/Cook Publishers, Inc., 1981).
12 Michael Polanyi, *Personal Knowledge: Towards a Post-Critical Philosophy* (Chicago: University of Chicago Press, 1958).
13 Berthoff, *The Making of Meaning*.
14 Sister Maria Thecia Hisrich and Father John M. Unger, A Sermon in Sculptured Stone and Jeweled Glass: Sacred Heart Church Commemorative Volume (Pittsburgh, PA: Printed in the United State, 1976).
15 Sam Keen and Anne Valley Fox, *Your Mythic Journey: Finding Meaning in Your Life through Writing and Story Telling* (New York: Putnam Publishing, 1989), 2.
16 William Shakespeare, "King Lear," in *The Complete Works of Shakespeare*, 3rd edition, ed. D. Bevington (Glenview, IL: Scott Foresman and Company, 1980/1605), Act 5, scene 3, lines 275-276.
17 Bartlett quoted in Kristie Fleckenstein, "Images, Words, and Narrative Epistemology," *College English*, 56, no. 8 (1996): 921.
18 Susan Langer, "Speculations on the Origins of Speech and its Communicative Function," in *Philosophical Sketches* (Baltimore: Johns Hopkins, 1962), 43.
19 Hample, *Memory and Imagination*, 701.
20 Ibid.

21 Heather McHugh spoken by Sam Hazo, Poetry Workshop Presentation (Pittsburgh, Pennsylvania: International Poetry Forum, 1999).
22 Carolyn Ellis, "Evocative Autoethnography: Writing Emotionally about Our Lives," in *Representation and The Text: Re-framing the Narrative Voice.*, ed. W. Tierney and Y. Lincoln (Albany: State University of New York, 1997), 117.
23 Fleckenstein, "Images, Words, and Narrative Epistemology," 921.
24 Hunter McEwan, "The Functions of Narrative and Research on Teaching," *Teaching and Teacher Education* 13, no. 1 (1997): 89.
25 Berthoff, *The Making of Meaning*, 4-5.
26 Frank Kermode, "Memory and Autobiography," *Raritan* 15, no. 1 (1995): 39.
27 Adrienne Rich, *On Lies, Secrets, and Silence: Selected Prose 1966-1978* (New York: W.W. Norton & Company, 1979).
28 Sue Johnston, "Images: A Way of Understanding the Practical Knowledge of Student Teachers," *Teaching and Teacher Education* 8, no. 2 (1992): 125.
29 C.A. Bowers, *The Promise of Theory: Education and Politics of Cultural Change* (New York: Teachers College Pres, 1987), 5.
30 Michael Connelly and Jean Clandinin, *Teachers as Curriculum Planners: Narratives of Experience* (New York: Teachers College Press, 1988), 60.
31 Fred A. Korthagen and Joseph Kessels, "Linking Theory and Practice: Changing the Pedagogy of Teacher Education," *Educational Researcher* (May 1999), 8.
32 Joseph Campbell with Bill Moyers, *The Power of Myth*, ed. B.S. Flowers (New York: Anchor Books, Doubleday, 1988).
33 Noreen Garman, "The Study of Educational Myth and Clinical Supervisory Practice" (paper presented at the annual meeting of The American Educational Research Association, Montreal, Canada, 1983).
34 Bowers, *The Promise of Theory*, 5.
35 Britzman, *Practice Makes Practice*, 5.
36 Willard Waller, *The Sociology of Teaching* (New York: John Wiley & Sons, Inc., 1932).
37 Edith Wharton, *Ethan Frome* (New York: Penguin Books, Ltd., Signet Classic, 1987), xiii.
38 Johnston, "Images: A Way of Understanding," 125.
39 Coleridge cited in Berthoff, *The Making of Meaning*.
40 Britzman, e-mail to author.
41 Shoshana Felman, "Psychoanalysis and Education: Teaching Terminable and Interminable," *Yale French Studies* no 63 (June 7, 1982).
42 Virginia Woolf, *A Room of One's Own* (Orlando, FL: Harcourt Brace Jovanovich, 1957/1929), 31.
43 Mary Doll, "Beyond the Window: Dreams and Learning," *Journal of Curriculum Theorizing* 4, no. 1 (1982), 199.
44 Felman, "Psychoanalysis and Education," 28.

45 Laurie Fincke, "Knowledge as Bait: Feminism, Voice and the Pedagogical Unconscious," *College English* 55, no. 1 (1991), 14.
46 Korthagen and Kessels, "Linking Theory to Practice."
47 Doll, "Beyond the Window," 198.
48 Ibid.
49 Patricia McMahon, "From Practice to Story to Research Text: The Role of Arts-based Research in Teacher Inquiry" (paper presented at The American Educational Research Association, Montreal, Canada, April 22, 1999), 22.
50 William Shakespeare, "Hamlet," in *The Complete works of Shakespeare*, 3rd edition, ed. D. Bevington (Glenview, IL: Scott Foresman and Company, 1980/1599), Act 2, scene 2, lines 255-257.
51 Jane Thompkins, "Look Back in Anger," *Teacher Magazine* (October 1996): 42.
52 Ibid., 43-44.
53 Ibid., 42.
54 Doll, "Beyond the Window," 198.
55 Deborah P. Britzman, "Cultural Myths in the Making of a Teacher: Biography and Social Structure in Teacher Education," *Harvard Educational Review* 56, no. 4 (1986): 448.
56 Ibid., 453.
57 Ibid., 451.
58 Britzman, *Practice Makes Practice*.
59 Robert V. Bullough and David K. Stokes, "Analyzing Personal Teaching Metaphors in Preservice Teacher Education as a Means for Encouraging Professional Development," *American Educational Research Journal* 31, no. 1 (1994): 199.
60 Ibid.
61 Nancy Sommers, "Between the Drafts," in *Women/Writing/Teaching*, ed. J.Z. Schmidt (Albany: State University of New York Press, 1998).

Essay Three

The Lanyard and the Whistle: Being an Authority

Maxine Greene believes that when we come to understand how things, truths, values are constituted for us, we will be able "to break some of the hold of the taken-for-granted," especially "the already constituted categories by which we interpret the world."[1] She talks about a time when we confront a world we have inherited when "already constituted" knowledge no longer rings true.

This is a time when we are no longer at ease with what we once believed; we feel that something is awry, something isn't quite right, but can't always name it. We sense a misfit, as if our favorite sweatshirt suddenly becomes too tight, begins to pull at the seams. In any case, what we once held as true comes into doubt, what once beckoned us as *the* way, becomes the wrong way or only one of several possible ways.

In this essay, I portray just such a time in my life. I talk about my coming to awareness of "already constituted categories," categories that connect gender roles with authority. I examine two episodes, "Summer Basketball Camp" and "The Playoff Game" that surface conflicts and contradictions around issues of being an authority. This writing then brings me to a place where I begin to realize "In every life there are experiences, painful and at first disorienting, which by their very intensity throw a sudden flashlight on the ways we have been living, the forces that control our lives, the hypocrisies that have allowed us to collaborate with those forces, the harsh but liberating facts we have been enjoined from recognizing." [2] My experiences start me along a way and to a time when I became "fierce with reality," as Florida Scott-Maxwell says, a new reality.[3]

SUMMER BASKETBALL CAMP

Each summer in the 1980s, Dave Schaffer and Jan Schmidt, directors of the R & M summer basketball camp for girls, invited me to join their coaching staff. Going to camp in those days was as much of a ritual for me as it was for the players. Always held in the last week of June, R & M gave me a chance to look forward to contests and games in gyms washed in sunlight instead of the darkness that shrouded gyms on game nights in February. At R & M, as I walked to the gym on the tree-lined paths of a college campus, memories of game nights and travel on drafty yellow school buses dimmed.

I particularly liked the first day of camp when anticipation and energy ran high, before the late nights and heat of days caused energy to wane. On the first day, Jan always handled one ritual—assigning campers to "stations" for competition and group drills. For these drills, a coach was positioned at the same basket each day and campers rotated with the "station" groups. Each coach taught a particular skill at her station—be it ball handling, rebounding, or shooting. I remember stations on one particular first day at R & M camp.

Jan had assigned me, along with Coach Joe, to the back or auxiliary gym. We R & M veterans called this the "baby gym" because of its size. Grade school age players were the only campers small enough to use this gym for games, but it sufficed for station drills. Since it was Joe's first year at camp, I took him to the baby gym as Jan explained the routine to the campers.

After Joe and I positioned ourselves at different baskets in the back gym, I remember looking back at the main gym. The campers sat huddled near the center jump circle, looking up at Jan as she gave instructions. I saw their faces, still clean and fresh, and I remembered why I liked first days. As I stood in the gym with a basketball in my hand and my whistle dangling from its lanyard, Jan signaled the beginning of stations and the campers were off and running to their baskets. (Camp rules said players had to sprint to and from each station.)

As the campers ran through the doors into the baby gym, I expected one group to gather around me at my basket. They never did. I clearly remember the silence that came when the squeak of tennis shoes stopped. At the same time, I looked on the scene to see that each little camper had run directly to Joe. From inside the tight circle that formed around him, I heard Joe say, "Girls, that's Coach Logsdon over there. I'm going to send half of you to her and then when the whistle blows, you'll switch baskets and come to me."

I remember feeling embarrassed and small. I stood alone, holding a basketball, feeling as if I had stolen it. A strong desire to flee filled me, yet my legs felt as if they were filled with sand. I couldn't move. I don't believe I was even able to turn and look away from what seemed to be an intimate scene between Joe and the young girls. As hard as I tried to overcome what I felt, to press it down, my feelings intensified—my face burned, my stomach sank. Run, leave, get out. I so wanted to not feel, to not see, but still I remained there, a witness, a spectator, awkwardly holding a basketball, feeling outside the scene, outside of myself. Joe smiled as he told the campers to come to me.

As I replay images of the scene, I clearly see him standing there and looking down at the campers, then pointing at me. I tried to overcome the pain I felt, and oddly the shame, too—shame that after a decade of coaching and ten years after Title IX, I still could not claim this title and this place at R & M. The age of these players, that they were so young, that they naturally and innocently ran to Joe—these things told me that in the minds of these young girls a coach was an "already constituted category" and the category was male. I may have carried the symbols of coach—the lanyard and the whistle—but I could not signify coach.

THE PLAYOFF GAME

I went to a playoff game to watch Center play Mt. Union. Each year Center, one of the best teams around, made the playoffs, but my own coaching schedule had always prevented me from seeing them play. Center had a reputation for playing good defense—my favorite aspect of the game. The coach, Coach Lang, had quite the reputation, too. I took my seat in the bleachers opposite the team benches so I had a clear view of the coaches, but I particularly wanted to watch Coach Lang to see what I could learn. The game promised to be a good one. Yet, what I was to see was both expected and not expected.

Throughout the game, Coach Lang yelled at her players and prowled the sideline, sometimes plopping down on the bench in disgust when a player failed to make a lay-up or threw the ball out-of-bounds. She pointed at players as they ran by and gestured for them to move this way or that way. Occasionally she paused to take a drink from a water bottle. One time when she removed one player from the game, she grabbed her by the shirt and screamed in her face. Another time, she followed a player to her seat on the bench and continued the harangue she had started when the player was in the game. As I watched, I heard comments from spectators who seemed to enjoy predicting Coach Lang's response to a particular situation or player. "Boy, will number 12 get it when she goes to that bench," or "You can bet number 10 won't do that again!" I heard other people proclaim, "My daughter would never play for her."

As I watched, I grew more and more uncomfortable. Coach Lang took player mistakes personally and the way she acted caught more and more of my attention as the game itself became a secondary drama. The coach displayed several qualities and faces. She portrayed distance and withdrawal when she plopped down on the bench, folded her arms across her chest, seeming to divorce herself from the game. She portrayed anger and disgust during time outs when she jutted her jaw, leaned into the circle of players who surrounded her, pointed and gestured in apparent displeasure. She portrayed sarcasm and ridicule when she stood up after an official made a call that went her team's way: "Fin – ally," she said with mock applause, extending her arms straight above her head and clapping.

As I watched I remember repeating to myself, "No, not me. I'm not that bad." I did a fast replay of my coaching behaviors, defending myself to myself. I didn't grab players by the shirt; I didn't berate them in public. *I* never looked like *that*. But something still troubled me. I felt a similarity. Why else would I have felt so guilty, so uncomfortable?

I think about the performance aspect of coaching and how coaches evoke spectator response. Begrudgingly acknowledged as "good," the Center coach either amused or angered people who watched her. I believe her behavior provoked amusement or anger because she appeared to cross boundaries in enacting a traditionally masculine role—coach. This *seeming* contradiction between her gender and her role drew attention to the incongruity of a female performing a masculine role in the same way that male actors must have created humor in Shakespearian comedies when they played female roles. When an audience went to the theater expecting a male to play a female role and the male actor then played a female character who donned a "disguise" as a male character, the gender masquerade and its comedic aspect were emphasized even more. This layering of gender roles highlighted the incongruity of "putting on" gender identity and "taking off" gender identity. In a similar way, TV personality Ru Paul, a male homosexual, "puts on" a female gender by wearing skyscraper heels, a tight dress and blonde wig, "cross-dressing" in an exaggerated portrayal of a "female persona." (Ru Paul compounds the identity portrayal by wearing a wig that seemingly "identifies" him as white or Caucasian, yet "he" is an African-American. By his portrayal of "Ru Paul," [Ru—a ruse?], he raises questions about the "gender," and "race" that "he" is or desires to be.)

Seen in another light, when Ru Paul cross-dresses or "puts on" gender, he shows, according to Butler, the way "Drag constitutes the mundane way in which genders are appropriated, theatricalized, worn and done." Butler contends that "all gendering is a kind of impersonation and approximation."[4] She posits a poststructuralist theory of gender as performance, and her theorizing adds to my interpretation of the ways that I and other spectators responded to Coach Lang.

The discomfort I felt as coach, woman, and spectator to Coach Lang's performance arose because of my contradictory position as woman and coach. Because the Center coach enacted a traditionally male role, albeit in the extreme—yelling and pacing the sideline, grabbing players, arguing with officials—she overemphasized "masculine" coaching behaviors and therefore drew more attention to the fact that a female was coaching. Like Ru Paul who may be perceived as "too" female in his attire and persona, Coach Lang was perceived as too "male" in her coaching. Her performance of coach seemed almost a caricature that highlighted normative roles and expectations, and like Ru Paul, caused extreme responses—either humor ("Boy, will number 12 get it when she goes to that bench.") or indignation ("My daughter would never play for her.")

Ferguson, in a reading of Butler, adds the summary that gender is not a fixed state, "but an on-going unstable process; one that involves performances by which an individual confirms or problematizes his or her gender to others."[5] So, when Butler claims that gender is not only performative but a *compulsory* performance in the sense that "acting out of line with heterosexual norms brings with it ostracism, punishment, and violence,"[6] it offers me the idea that Coach Lang's behavior involved a "performance" that problematized her gender because of the role she assumed. And, even though Butler frames her discussion about homosexuality, her comments may be applied to this coaching context as well. She contends that cross-dressing or homosexuality is "acting out of line" with heterosexual norms and may cause violent or extreme response. The spectator response to Coach Lang provoked either humor or indignation because a woman who acted "coach," acted a "male" role and violated cultural expectations.

In addition to this, when I consider what it means to be indignant, I think of it as a moral response that closes the door on any kind of illumination. The indignant person already stands within the room of the righteous, closing out others. I was appalled at Coach Lang's behavior and my response was to condemn her, to "collaborate" as Rich would say with the very forces that influenced the campers to run directly to Joe; forces that also compelled me to "become enjoined" with them.[7] Thus, my indignation. How could she act this way? Yet, at the same time, as much as I said, "Not me," I saw myself in her.

Coach Lang, as a mirror image, surfaced contradictions and conflicts within me. I, too, was given to tantrums. I, too, performed. So, while R & M caused me to doubt what I felt and felt *entitled* to (perhaps surfaced doubts that had been there all along), watching Coach Lang caused me to see and not to see. This doubled vision shaped by a "doubled consciousness" that Gilligan[8] and other feminists say is prevalent among females, caused me to disassociate in destructive ways. Viewing myself through the eyes of others as Griffin says, made me disown a part of myself. She says, "We grow used to ignoring the evidence of our own experience, what we hear or see, what we feel in our bodies."[9] In being a spectator to the way a role was "put on" and put on in an unacceptable way, I showed an awareness of how "coach" was constructed in the discourses of the community. Because I couldn't see how else to construct coach, because my inner vision failed, I collaborated with the normative. Rather than resolve the gender problematic, I vowed that I would never act or preform "coach" in the way Coach Lange enacted coach.

Thus, my response was to modify my coaching behavior. I eliminated "masculine" behaviors and accentuated feminine qualities. I wore dresses and heels instead of slacks that would have been more comfortable and practical. I attempted to remove or "cover" the "masculine" aspects of the coaching role. I focused on keeping my gestures and behavior feminine. But, what I really tried to make over were what I perceived as "masculine" aspects of myself, those gendered qualities (in coaching) that until this time were associated with males. Not realizing then what I realize now—that identity may be fluid and multiple, that gender, as Butler asserts is always an imitation, a performance, I played out, much as Ru Paul does, an exaggerated portrayal of the feminine.[10] Of course the irony is that in doing this I became much like the actors in the Shakespearean comedies who donned a "disguise" that portrayed their actual sexual identity. In other words, although my sexual gender is female, I felt somehow I needed to be more "female" because the role I enacted as coach was considered masculine. Thus, if I covered the masculine aspects, I would not look like Coach Lang, nor would I feel uncomfortable. I looked at gender and gender roles in a simple and modernist way. I coded behaviors and attitudes either male or female. While I *felt* ambiguities and contradictions, my attempts to resolve these ambiguities were external, cosmetic in an ironic way.

If I had recognized that Coach Lang claimed her title of coach and in doing this was entitled to "put on" behavior, be it foolish or authoritarian, I may have been able to claim the aspect of my identity that caused my ambivalence—female and coach. Put another way, my discomfort came from conflating role with identity. Whereas role "speaks to public function" or what one is supposed to do, identity voices "subjective investments and commitments."[11] But as Blumenthal notes, we believe in and still construct a humanist self which is singular and cohesive. (I say we *resist* identity that is shifting and seek to maintain a cohesive self.)

According to Blumenthal, I was locked into the *schema* aspect of identity and located my coaching identity in the images that I had of coach which were masculine.[12] While I was *assigned* or labeled within my institution within a role position (coach), my personal as well as the collective image of "coach" remained male. Thus, I embodied contradictory conceptions of the gendered nature of being a coach and being an authority. I lived what Walkerdine calls, "an impossible fiction,"[13] since the social construct of coach was male and I am female.

If I had recognized when Coach Lang filed suit to receive salary equal to the male coaches in her district, that she saw Title IX of the Educational Amendments (1972) as legal recourse to affirm her right not only to "wear" or assume the role and title of coach, but equity as well, then I may have been able to view "coach" as an "already constituted category."[14] But this was not my response. I felt excluded from the category coach because my subjectivity had already been formed by what Bloom calls "prevailing discourses."[15] Because I did not yet have an understanding of ways to construct an identity or subjectivity as shifting or multiple, I was unable to challenge the construct of coach as male. Had I been able to accept a more tentative and "internally persuasive discourse," as Britzman describes it,"[16] I might have eventually found a more comfortable place to be with myself as a coach. But, I was only prepared to interpret my experiences against the backdrop of the dominant discourse, not the discourse that spoke of resistance.

But more than this, I agreed with the prevailing "logic" of the discourse of this time that said girls' sports did not attract the same type of public attention and scrutiny as boys' high school sports, so female coaches did not deserve pay equal to male coaches. It was assumed that female athletic events would simply never attract the same crowds or be as popular as male sports, even with equal money for scholarships. Therefore male coaches "earned" more pay. Also, in a paternalistic sentiment, if females wanted equal pay with males, then they would also have to accept the pressures attendant to the coaching role and would also have to put their jobs on the line. Firing male coaches or pressuring them to resign was not uncommon in high school athletics according to the talk of the time. Why would women want this kind of equality?

So, in light of these discourses and my own inability to resist the way gender and "coach" were constructed, I found myself feeling inadequate in terms of authority also. If I couldn't' enact coach as it was constructed as male, then neither could I assume the expert authority that attached itself to this construct. I felt this when the R & M campers ran directly toward Joe, when they saw two adults in the gym, both wearing coaching symbols, the lanyard and the whistle, both assigned the title of coach. Still, the campers ran to

Joe. He "naturally" occupied the subject position of coach. I did not. If being a coach means performing a role in the public arena as well as possessing knowledge that enables one to enact this role (knowledge that separates "coach" from "not coach"), and if I accept Welker's notion of expert as someone who has "acquired a special knowledge that is not widely shared" that allows the expert "to provide a service," then I was an "expert."[17] Yet, more than a decade after Title IX of the Educational Amendments became law, providing equivalent access to facilities and equal pay for females in athletics, I still could not claim the *meaning* of coach or be what coach signified. Cultural beliefs die hard. The legal script of Title IX had not erased the cultural script. The young campers at R & M taught me this. Coach Lang showed me this. In coming to this awareness, still tacit at the time, I felt the burden of playing a role that was a contradiction. While I was "in authority," I could not be "an authority."

Thus, denied expert authority, I could only "put on" a coach identity; I was not entitled to it. I felt inadequate, impotent, "deauthorized" because of the cultural assumptions about the way coach was constructed.[18] In retrospect, I now understand why I worked so hard at being a coach and always fell short of my expectations. I was never good enough. I attended clinics, read books, talked to other coaches, never ceased from expecting more of myself in terms of understanding basketball. I never simply watched a game—I *studied* games. In short, I did everything to compensate for my lack. Yet, no matter what recognition I received; no matter what record I achieved, I believed I was never good enough. Until I could come to understand the "impossible fiction"[19] I lived, and see identity construction in a different way, I could never be comfortable with myself. In assuming the role of coach, I occupied a position of ambivalence, outside the discourse, and yet paradoxically, inside. If subjectivity is constructed through language and discourse as Bloom and Weedon suggest,[20] then my trying to enact "coach" that was both feminine and masculine, was an apparent contradiction. Coaching for me became as Gans describes, a "constant strain" because of my "marginal" position.[21]

I think back now to a comment my mother made to me after a tightly contested game where I was particularly animated and vocal. It throws another light on my coaching behaviors and how I didn't meet her expectations. After the game she stopped to chat and congratulate me. In the quiet and measured tones she used for matters of import, she asked, "Marjorie, do you have to yell?" My glib response, "Only if I want to be heard, mother," hid the complex and contradictory nature of my attempts to claim the position of coach and expert. Because my "either/or" thinking viewed yelling, and certain other behaviors, as part and parcel of being a coach—at least as I had seen it at games or on TV—I reasoned that if I couldn't yell, I couldn't coach. My mother though had expectations of how I would preform this role as did the spectators of the Center coach. After I saw the Center coach and heard the damning comments, my image of female coach changed. The line, "Her voice was ever so soft, Gentle and low"—a favorite of Sr. Mercuri and my mother—framed coach, woman, feminine, masculine in definitive ways. My glib response at this time in my early career as coach, hid the gendered nature of coach and the gendered nature of authority in ways that continue to play out in the high school coaching arena.

Two years ago, a girls' high school basketball coach, Suzie McConnell-Serio, made national headlines in *USA Today*, as well as television appearances on the *Today* and *Rosie O'Donnell* shows. The reason for her appearance was because she left a high school basketball game to be rushed to the hospital to deliver a baby. While Coach McConnell-Serio, a former two-time Olympic champion and Women's National Basketball League player is a prominent sports figure, her basketball celebrity garnered national attention with this event.

It seems to me that her basketball status was made more acceptable or was justified by her motherhood. Could it be, as Pronger suggests, that not only "was and is the entire structure" of sports in the schools and in society generally "masculine" in nature, but that sport "produces a particular version of maleness and femaleness, a version which glorifies the former at the expense of the latter."[22]

Pursuing this further suggests that females need to compensate for the maleness of their athleticism. In the McConnll-Serio instance, the media rushed to emphasize the "femaleness" of giving birth. In this way, public discourses "conceal their own invention" as Foucault says."[23]

I'm thinking now, too, about how years after my mother asked if I needed to yell during games, our athletic director said, "As a coach, you were always our best teacher." My immediate and visceral response was to recoil. I didn't like what he said. Now I realize why. The comment really said that I could teach, a subject position available to me as a woman, but I couldn't coach, a subject position I occupied and yet could not occupy.

SPECULATIONS ON AUTHORITY

I realize now that the contradictions that I felt but left unexamined and *unchallenged* gave me the "maneuverability of a straightjacket" as Knowles says in *A Separate Peace*, in terms of the way I constructed subjectivity and authority. I framed gendered behaviors for coach as masculine or feminine, as did the spectators, my mother, Sr. Mercuri, and Fr. Stokely. This excluded me from positions of authority and also locked me into a binary thinking about gender. Now I assume that any gendered identity is neither fixed nor unitary, and that multiple identities are just that, multiple, not fragmented.[24] Now I realize that I accepted an "already constituted category," and it was male. But in the 1980s, I denied my feelings of exclusion, knew that to act in non-feminine ways invited the same kind of response or insinuation about gender that lurked beneath the criticisms of Coach Lang. Why did a woman coach like a man?

NOTES

1. Maxine Greene, "The Lived World," in the *Education Feminist Reader*, ed. R. Stone (New York: Routledge, 1994), 19.
2. Adrienne Rich, *On Lies, Secrets, and Silences: Selected Prose 1966-1978* (New York: W.W. Norton & Company, 1979), 215.
3. Florida Scott-Maxwell, quoted in Parker J. Palmer, *The Courage to Teach: Exploring the Inner Landscape of a Teacher's Life* (San Francisco: Jossey-Bass Publishers, 1998), 29.
4. Judith Butler, "Imitation and Gender Insubordination," in *Women, Knowledge, and Reality: Explorations in Feminist Philosophy*, ed. A. Garry and M. Pearsall (New York: Routledge, 1966), 378.
5. Ann Ferguson, "Can I Choose Who I Am? And How Would that Empower Me? Gender, Race, Identities and the Self," in *Women, Knowledge, and Reality: Explorations in Feminist Philosophy*, ed. A. Garry and M. Pearsall (New York: Routledge, 1966), 111.
6. Butler, "Imitation and Gender Insubordination," 381.
7. Rich, *On Lies, Secrets, and Silence*.
8. Carol Gilligan, *In a Different Voice: Psychological Theory and Women's Development* (Cambridge, MA: Harvard University Press, 1982).
9. Susan Griffin, "Split Culture," in *The Schumacher Series*, ed. S. Kumin (London: Blonde & Briggs, 1984), 175.
10. Butler, "Imitation and Gender Insubordination."
11. Deborah Britzman, "Is There a Problem with Knowing Thyself? Toward a Poststructuralist View of Teacher's Identity," in *Teachers Thinking, Teachers Knowing*, ed. T. Shanahan (Urbana, IL: National Conference on Research in English, 1994), 59.
12. Dannielle Blumenthal, "Representations of the Divided Self," in *Qualitative Inquiry* 5, no 3 (1999).
13. Valerie Walkerdine, "Progressive Pedagogy and Political Struggle," in *Feminism and Critical Pedagogy*, ed. C. Luke and J. Gore New York, Routledge, 1992).
14. Maxine Greene, "The Lived World."
15. Leslie Bloom, *Under the Sign of Hope: Feminist Methodology and Narrative Interpretation* (Albany: State University of New York Press, 1998), 64.
16. Britzman, "Is There a Problem with Knowing Thyself?"
17. Robert Welker, *The Teacher as Expert: A Theoretical and Historical Examination* (Albany: State University of New York Press, 1992).
18. Carmen Luke, "Feminist Pedagogy Theory: Reflections on Power and Authority," *Educational Theory* 46, no 1 (1996).
19. Walkerdine, "Progressive Pedagogy and Political Struggle."

20 The construction of subjectivity through language and discourse is developed by Bloom, *Under the Sign of Hope* and by Chris Weedon, *Feminist Practice and Poststructuralist Theory* (Oxford, London: Blackwell Publishers, 1987).
21 H.J. Gans, "The Participant-Observer as a Human Being: Observations on the Personal Aspects of Field Work," in *Institutions and Person: Papers Presented to Everett C. Huges*, ed. H.S. Becker, B. Geer, D. Riesman, and R.S. Weiss (Chicago: Aldine, 1968).
22 Pronger quoted in William Pinar, William M. Reynolds, Patrick Slattery, and Peter M. Taubman, *Understanding Curriculum: An Introduction to the Study of Historical and Contemporary Discourses* (New York: Peter Lang Publishers, Inc., 1995), 363.
23 Foucault quoted in Robin Usher and Richard Edwards, *Postmodernism and Education* (New York: Routledge, 1994), 90.
24 My view of gendered identity is influenced by the following: Bloom, *Under the Sign of Hope*; Weedon, *Feminist Practice and Poststructuralist Theory*; Teresa de Lauretis, *Technologies of Gender: Essays on Theory, Film, and Fiction* (Indiana: Indiana University Press, 1987).

Essay Four

Turning Toward Portfolios and Writing: Sharing Authority

THE CONVERT

Conversion may have struck Paul of Tarsus like a bolt of lightning, rudely dumping him from his horse, but I suspect that before this abrupt "call," Paul had hints of revelations coming to him all along the road. Something brought him to this place, this crossroad. Perhaps he had been particularly good at ignoring warning signs, particularly reluctant to change—most of us are. "Why abandon a belief" as Frost says, merely "because it ceases to be true."[1] Changing a habit or a profession involves risks that leave us riding that same old horse down the same old paths, leads us to ignore signs and symbols until something finally jars us enough to throw us off our familiar mounts.

"Probably there are hordes of us" who walk around ignoring a call, "professing" something that doesn't hold true for us anymore (or perhaps never did)"[2] We ignore too the "feelings of bodily and emotional stress because of the disembodiment involved in how we are taught to teach, to learn, and to do research."[3] But, we possess a "tacit knowledge," a knowing that we cannot initially explain because it is visceral and internal.[4] Our bodies tell us, Heshusius and Ballard say, but we repress "somatic awareness"; we get headaches or "cover up the stress caused by the disembodiment of our work by still more work, or by still another cup of coffee."[5] So, even though *in our bones* we may realize something is troubling, we often spend a lifetime listening to the voice of custom that beckons us "Stay."

This is the way it happened with me. Cultivating a kind of studied ignorance I busied myself in the day to day cascade of events that compose a teacher's life. Critical moments came and went. Yet I still practiced the same beliefs, still denied the knowledge of my senses. Reflection was no stranger to me, but it was reflection on the *how* of pedagogy, not the *why* that lay behind the practice. (Why abandon a belief?)

Even though mother-like I had ignored the tug of doubt at the sleeve of my practice, meeting Professor N and beginning a doctoral program made me pause and re-examine my teaching. I looked back on troubling moments that I had denied, began to question what makes knowledge and what makes a teacher. When this happened, new understandings began to inform my pedagogy, particularly about how I perceived my authority as an English teacher and teacher of composition.

Changing approaches to writing, especially when I added narrative and portfolios to the curriculum, altered how I perceived my relationship with students. When they wrote about their experiences, I learned to acknowledge the authority of their texts. This understanding also led me to approach literature and classroom practice in other ways. Teaching then became an act of composing a "discipline of writing" with students, a co-authoring if you will, rather than imposing content on them.

Thus, what I portray here are paths I've traveled as an English teacher set against a "biography of the discipline,"[6] a story of my life as a teacher of English (necessarily partial and incomplete) set against a story of the discipline of English (also partial and incomplete). I show how altering the content of what I teach influences my role as an authority, causes me to desire to "share" my authority with students. I show how after years of teaching, conversion, which had followed me along the way, finally caught me, made me turn and turn again—a turning *from* former authoritarian practices and a turning *toward* a pedagogy of personal authority.

PULPITS

Smug. Even in my own ears I sounded smug. Realizing self-righteousness held me in its grip. Still I didn't stop myself and elect for a more judicious tone. No. Once I climbed my pulpit, pronouncements most surely would follow. "Kath-ee," I said to my friend and fellow English teacher (with a heavy tone of impatience, I'm sure), "our students write *thesis* papers; they don't write *personal* narratives." It was 1994 and we were returning from the convention of the National Council of English Teachers.

At Catholic, I explained, students didn't write journals, didn't hand in revisions, didn't "do" personal writings. (Freshmen may have written a few narratives, but upper level students learned "higher order" thinking.) Perhaps students in her *public* school did those things, but our English department challenged our students with *academic* writing, with rigorous thinking. We taught critical writing, beginning with the traditional five paragraph essay and working up to a literary research paper.

Even as I professed the superiority of thesis writing to Kathy, I recollect feeling a tinge of regret. I heard how I sounded and something told me I would regret what I said, but, as the old song says, "Fools rush in," so I persisted in voicing the superiority of thesis writing and our curriculum. I stuck to my "position" the same way my students often stick to theirs. (Why should knowledge interfere with an opinion" is what I often say to *them* when *they* are particularly dogmatic.) I knew our tradition had roots in the teachings of the Jesuits and didn't everyone respect the Jesuits? (The *Ratio Studiorum* in 1586, a plan of study initiated by the Jesuits "affirmed the value of classical study, the transmission of the accumulated wisdom of Western culture and . . . emphasized training in logical argument: thesis, evidence, objections, discussion, final proof."[7])

In short, our English curriculum at Catholic, modeled on the Jesuit *Ratio*, emphasized the student's ability to reason, an intellectual development deemed necessary to grasp understandings about person, society, and God.[8] Because we at Catholic, like many English teachers in the 1950s, 60s, and 70s, were trained as literary critics first and teachers of literature second, we also embraced one form of writing, believing that the literary thesis was the best evidence of a student's ability to reason and think logically.[9] In *The Rise and Fall of English*, Scholes notes:

> THIS MEANT THAT THE WRITTEN TEXTS PRODUCED BY STUDENTS WERE OF A VASTLY DIFFERENT KIND FROM THE IMAGINATIVE TEXTS STUDIED IN CLASS. INSTEAD OF READING ORATIONS AND PRODUCING ORATORY (HISTORICALLY THE WAY THE DISCIPLINE OF ENGLISH EVOLVED) STUDENTS BEGAN TO READ LITERATURE AND PRODUCE CRITICISM—AND THE STAGE WAS SET FOR THE TWENTIETH-CENTURY DEVELOPMENTS IN THE FIELD OF ENGLISH. THIS SAME PROCESS, OF COURSE, HAD TRANSFORMED THE STUDENTS FROM PRODUCERS OF WORK COMPARABLE TO WHAT THEY STUDIED INTO PASSIVE CONSUMERS OF TEXTS THEY COULD NEVER HOPE TO EMULATE—CHANGING THE TEACHER INTO A MIDDLEMAN, HUCKSTER, OR PRIESTLY EXEGETE.[10]

WRITING FRAGMENTS

Looking back to the early 1980s, I remember when English department policy required that we fail any student if one fragment or run-on sentence sullied her paper, regardless of the quality of her ideas. At first I followed the policy, but later compromised and began to give two grades expressed in a fraction, the upper grade for content, the lower grade for grammar and written expression. Our curriculum emphasized literature, so we didn't dedicate much time to grammar, or writing and the composing process, (even though Emig's seminal study on writing as process had been published in 1971).[11] We demanded that our students "produce" papers that were grammatically correct. Students were to write thesis papers on literary topics; we graded them. Our "corrections" really were intended to justify the grade or show "where we took off points" since revising and re-grading papers was not an aspect of our pedagogy. I suppose we subscribed to what Young calls a "vitalist" assumption: no one can really teach anyone else how to write.[12]

By subscribing to this type of curriculum, we assumed a role of evaluators and judges—not teachers—of writing. Janet Emig, president of the National Council of English Teachers in 1989 talks about a realization that she made which speaks to what we did at Catholic:

> RATHER EARLY ON IT OCCURRED TO ME WHAT WAS GOING ON IN SCHOOLS WAS NOT THE TEACHING OF WRITING; IT WAS RATHER THE ASSIGNING AND THEN THE GRADING OF WRITING, WITH THIS GRAND CANYON BETWEEN. NO ONE WAS EXPLORING HOW WE GOT FROM HERE TO THERE, AND SO THE ONLY PEOPLE WHO FARED WELL IN THIS WERE THOSE WHO COULD ALREADY WRITE. THIS IS A BIZARRE WAY OF PROCEEDING.[13]

I remember how we English teachers lamented that students simply no longer understood good grammar or correct sentence structure. We sought (and found) "research" that confirmed how ineffective it was to teach grammar to high school students, even as we snubbed the paradigm shift from product to process writing. (In the final report from the Anglo-American Seminar on the Teaching of English held at Dartmouth College in 1966, the scholars agreed that the formal teaching of grammar and usage should be de-emphasized so that students could engage in the writing process in a non-prescriptive atmosphere."[14] Experience taught us that teaching grammar simply didn't work. Students who could perform well doing "exercises" or "skills" and identify fragments or run-on sentences continued to sprinkle incorrect sentences into their writing. Armed with "expert" opinion and frustrated by our pedagogical failure, we voiced sentiments in a "pass the blame down to teachers before us," kind of mentality that asserted if students didn't know grammar and sentence structure by the time they got to us, there was nothing more we could do. In this way of thinking, Scholes would agree that we remained much like other English teachers:

> THESE, LET US REMEMBER, WERE THE GOOD OLD DAYS, AND WHAT WE LEARN FROM THEM IS THAT FROM 1770 TO 1914 AND RIGHT ON TO THE PRESENT MOMENT, ENGLISH TEACHERS HAVE NOT FOUND ANY METHOD TO ENSURE THAT GRADUATES OF THEIR COURSES WOULD USE WHAT THEY CONSIDERED TO BE CORRECT GRAMMAR AND SPELLING. . . [AND] WE MAY WELL BE CONTEMPLATING TWO HUNDRED YEARS OF WASTED EFFORT.[15]

Thus, we enforced a policy that made the students solely responsible for their writing or revisions. We stood outside the process of composing and even more significantly, since we espoused only a pedagogy of correcting, we omitted a pedagogy of composing. In doing this we conveyed an idea that writers were born not made. Good writing was something one could or couldn't do naturally. As teachers who graded student writing, we took a God-like stance toward assessment (which must have made our "ways" seem very much like God's, mysterious and powerful). No wonder students often said that they just couldn't write. In saying this, they had accepted our assessments and learned to value themselves through our eyes. We, after all, were the authorities, the judges, who knew best.

STUDENTS WRITING

"*This* time it's really, really good," Maureen exclaims. Looking up from the paper in my hand I say, "Great. As soon as I'm finished with Jamie, I'll be right over." She sits at her desk and wears a "Wait until you get-a-load of this look." Pleased with her writing, her tone of voice and her look say that this time she "got it"; she knows it, and she doesn't need me to affirm it so much as she wants me to share in her triumph. It is 1998. My students are writing personal narratives, and I am teaching Creative Writing.

CREATIVE WRITING

After returning from a sabbatical, I find a new class listed on my schedule for the first semester of 1993—Creative Writing. I hear that students had lobbied for the course and it is added for this semester. Because I served as advisor to the yearbook and newspaper, the department decided that I am the logical choice to teach the class. And so, I become the creative writing teacher. While experience with yearbook copy helps get me through the first year, my experiences at the university, particularly with portfolios, will alter me in ways that became visible through my teaching.

A "PORTFOLIO" FINAL

Professor N taught several curriculum and qualitative research courses at the university. She was announcing that a portfolio would be required for our final in "Curriculum and the Adult Learner." (*Good, I think immediately—something different. This may light something in me.*) Like the other graduate students in the class, I wonder what I will write and what portfolios are supposed to show. Like the other graduate students, I had expected the final would be some sort of twenty page research paper, just like all the other papers I had written before I dropped the Ph.D. program in literature at another university. But Professor N doesn't do what I expect. We will submit a portfolio for our final "assessment." It is the summer of 1992.

PORTFOLIOS 1

"But, how long should it be?" (Graduate student, Curriculum and the Adult Learner, 1992)

"Can we see a model portfolio so we can get a clearer picture of what you want?" (Graduate student, Curriculum and the Adult Learner, 1992)

In answer to a veritable litany of questions, Professor N responds, (but in a much kinder and more patient way that I summarize here). Length—whatever is appropriate for ideas. Models—not appropriate—consider your learning, not someone else's. Yes, you may "research" a topic suggested through the readings, but you don't have to proceed that way. (I smile and think to myself how the questions students ask teachers have a universal and often highly neurotic quality.) Well, she explains, portfolios show the way of one's thinking. And yes, they display one's work. (*Hey, it's summer time; my sabbatical year yawns in front of me. I'll figure it out.*)

PORTFOLIOS II

Portfolios may demonstrate many things, Professor N explains. Approaches may show "the development of thinking or understanding over time. . ., [or] understanding of the many facets of a given concept, topic, or issue, [or] reflect an individual's values, world view or philosophical questions."[16] She talks a lot about meaning and "sense making." The portfolio, in other words, may be academically solid, and at the same time be original and creative. In portraying the processes by which a student produces work, portfolios also offer rationale and reflection that seek to capture the meta-cognitive.[17]

Hooked. I am definitely hooked. I can make this mine, my meanings, not someone else's. Vitality. She is talking about portfolio writing and vitality. What to make of this? I am excited and immediately begin to think about how portfolios will work in my classes. As I think about authoring a portfolio that best represents *my understandings* of the course content, that I don't have to perform on a test or write a paper with standard Modern Language Association format, I feel as if I have died and gone to heaven.

PORTFOLIO NOTES I

I still have the hand written note with Professor N's assessment of my portfolio dated 1992. She comments on my "continual coming to terms" with the shifting language of curriculum. She accepts how I speak of my changing epistemology and reminds me to "Speak of the world's own change."[18] Her personalized note acknowledges that I am okay, that grappling with language, with anti-foundationalist concepts of knowledge expresses the "world view" I embrace. ("Where my feet are planted," she says.) It is okay that I am just beginning to understand assumptions about learning and knowledge and how metaphors shape or describe curriculum. ("Language is world making," she says, quoting Wittgenstein. Years later, each time I show the film *Il Postino* in my World Literature class, I smile, because now I understand what Mario means when he says, "You mean the whole world is a metaphor for something else?" He was awakening to the language of poetry; to ways language makes the world.)

Portfolio Notes II

After adding portfolios and narrative approaches to my classes in both Creative Writing and World Literature, the content and tone of my notes on student papers change. I find myself saying, "I like your revision and how your focus moves to the commonplace. Good. We sometimes forget that life exists in the ordinary." My "pedagogy of correcting" where my authority was final and irrevocable begins to turn to a "pedagogy of composing" where my authority rests within a negotiated or shared construction of writing.

In student drafts I say things like: "I enjoyed your revisions—particularly about your room and your locker. I would like to see more of your room (I know it is pink and white), especially the posters and pictures that make it yours. In a similar way, the locker becomes the symbol for your school life—the conversations, laughs, secrets that happen there. This, too, has potential to develop into something else. Keep working on your writing. You're doing fine."

I hear a difference in what I write on student papers. I begin a conversation, use pronouns you, your, and I. A person and a voice come through my notes, and I feel that the distance between myself and my students diminishes. Where I once commented on "cogent" arguments, "excellent use of textural examples" (comments from above), I now speak about writing as "never really finished." Try this, I urge. Let's see what happens. I express uncertainty and "where the writing will go" until I "hear" it. I am amazed when *I* begin to hear *my* voice in what I write on papers. I revise "myself" and my God-like stance, realizing that we don't always know what we will say before we say it; that the traditional paradigm doesn't work for narrative and other forms of writing; that expository writing assumes an unchanging reality independent of the writer, expresses a view I am coming to reject, an authoritative stance I am abandoning.[19] Composing *with* students causes me to vacate the role of judge; my role as an authority changes. I enter into the process of writing with students, a process we share, an authority we share; a process where understandings unfold from the very act of writing.

PORTFOLIO NOTES III

A student writes: "I wrote my autobiography out of order, which seemed to help me sort out my thoughts. I did sections that were not upsetting first and left the most painful until the end." No outlines. No lockstep thesis point one, "proof a, b and c." I begin to understand that writing is recursive.[20] I see it. I hear it in what students say in their reflections in portfolios. (*As I write this essay and this dissertation, I come to an even deeper meaning of recursive, of "writing out of order," of thinking that circles me back to other places in the text, of new ways to approach texts.*)

When a student writes, "Enjoy writing? I don't think I have ever used the word 'enjoy' to describe writing. I don't hate it, but I don't love it either," I see that she shares her thoughts about writing with me. This is okay. She says that she is "better at writing something when it comes from the heart, and not when it is forced." I believe her. I understand. Her text is authored by her understanding of experience. The text we construct together through various drafts and revisions makes the process dialogic. I am "in it" with her. I still advise her, but I listen to her resistance to my comments if she expresses resistance. She makes her case; I make mine. We negotiate. We navigate the waters of ambiguity together. But since writing is not permanent, neither are my assessments. Revisions are always accepted. Grades are not final because revision continues; our conversations continue.

PORTFOLIO NOTES IV

"It was like my subconscious needed me to write this and when I did, I felt a weight lifted from my shoulders," Mandy says. She speaks about making the unconscious conscious.[21] She writes her life, or a part of it. *I understand. I am writing mine, too.* I discover I can't be the same teacher anymore, not in relationship to how I enact authority. I no longer simply grade papers with the only "conversation" written in the margin as corrections—"awk," "sp," "diction." (*I think now that there is no "correct" in terms of ideas, and there are multiple ways to express understandings. Knowledge is personal and subjective; my experience matters.*) We are in a process together. I don't have all of the answers. Some. I have some. When students compose narratives of their lives, grading takes on another dimension. I struggle with ways to affirm their experience and get them to understand that they write for an audience (a concern that dictates a need for clarity and obedience to conventions). Together we struggle to negotiate lives—theirs and mine; experiences—theirs and mine; written expression and assessment. I discover that the texts we create through the writing process shape authority—theirs and mine. It is an authority that circulates between my students and myself; an authority we construct along with the content of the writing. It is an authority shared; an authority that shapes my pedagogy and my teacher subjectude.

SPECULATIONS ON SHARING AUTHORITY

By converting to a pedagogy of sharing authority, I assumed a missionary zeal in spreading the message of my new beliefs. (What's a conversion worth if we can't preach the error of someone else's ways? Didn't Paul convert from persecuting Christians to increasing their number?)

I spoke to my colleagues about portfolio and narrative writing, euphorically proclaiming the merits of these types of writing. Soon our department adopted portfolio assessment for the English curriculum. Spreading the word served to increase my zeal and decrease my critical appraisal of what new approaches meant to my pedagogy and "my authority. Still, I became the disciple of the portfolio.

In coming to realize that my past practices and approaches to "thesis" papers took "objective" knowledge for granted—a knowledge that is discoverable and separate from the author—I began to question the sole use of the "thesis" or expository approach to writing; a writing that expects each student to describe things in the same way.[22] Once I viewed knowledge as subjective, made through the experience of the author, shaped through discursive practices, I began to understand how language *is* world making. I affirmed my experience, named the new ways I perceived myself in relationship with students, named my self as "sharing authority" with them. When I used this language to speak of my changing notions of authority, I was beginning to discover what Schwandt means when he says:

> MOREOVER, THE SIGNIFICANCE OF OUR LANGUAGE USE DOES NOT RESIDE SOLELY IN ITS CAPACITY TO DESIGNATE, DISCOVER, REFER, OR DEPICT ACTUAL STATES OF AFFAIRS. RATHER, LANGUAGE IS USED TO CARRY OUT OR PERFORM ACTIONS, TO DISCLOSE HOW THINGS ARE PRESENT TO US AS WE DEAL WITH THEM. THIS IS THE HISTORICAL, CULTURAL, AND LINGUISTIC CONTEXT OF OUR PRACTICES. . .WE BOTH START AND END OUR EFFORTS TO ANSWER THE QUESTION "WHAT DO WE MAKE OF THIS?" IN OUR BEST GRASP, OUR BEST ACCOUNT, OF OURSELVES AS AGENTS IN THE WORLD. [23]

Thus, my new use of language to describe authority, formed by new understandings of knowledge and the discipline of teaching composition, compelled me to act in different ways. New metaphors shaped my understanding of teacher and learner. (As Elbow notes, "[W]e tend to get more of our unconscious into our discourse when we use metaphors and tell stories."[24]) Overturning the traditional writing paradigm (the product approach) meant that I encouraged students to share writing with me, that I valued their comments and observations. My relationship with students shifted. What I thought of their role in the learning process changed, too. I used a metaphor by Adrienne Rich on my course descriptions that urges students in "claiming an education"[25] and discussed with them what this idea might mean in terms of their involvement in learning. (They were not at Catholic to "get" an education; neither were they little banks into which teachers made deposits, as Freire noted.[26]) When I read feminist theory, I nodded in agreement about valuing experience, allowing the personal into the classroom, especially through writing.

But what I'm coming to realize through the writing is that I assumed that authority was something I possessed and could "hand over" to students. The metaphor, like teaching itself, assumes an active and receptive participant. I assumed (like most converts) that students would readily embrace my new beliefs and practices, discard their former beliefs with élan. Even as I struggled to relinquish authoritarian practices (authority practiced for its own sake, says Burbules[27]), I assumed that all students would automatically click their heels and come skipping merrily after me—become the converts I wanted them to be. How could they fail to see how participation and open communication would benefit them? Forgetting how long and arduous the journey was for me, forgetting that not all baptisms are of water, I assumed that all students would embrace conversion as I did.

NOTES

1. Robert Frost, "The Black Cottage," in *A Pocket Book of Robert Frost's Poems* (New York: Washington Square Press, 1964), 12.
2. Lous Heshusius and Keith Ballard, "How Do We Count the Ways We Know" Some Background to the Project," in *From Positivism to Interpretivism and Beyond: Tales of Transformation in Educational and Social Theory (The Mind Body Connection)*, ed. L Heshusius and K Ballard (New York: Teachers College Press, 1996).
3. Ibid., 3.
4. Michael Polanyi, *The Tacit Dimension* (London: Routledge & Kegan, 1966).
5. Heshusius and Ballard, "How Do We Count the Ways We Know?" 3.
6. Kathleen M. Ceroni, e-mail to author, July 2000.
7. Anthony S. Bryk, Valerie E. Lee, and Peter B. Holland, *Catholic Schools and the Common Good* (Cambridge, MA: Harvard University Press, 1993), 19.
8. Ibid., 31.

9   Maxine Hairston, "The Winds of Change: Thomas Kuhn and the Revolution in Teaching Writing," in *Landmark Essays on Writing Process*, ed. S. Perl (Davis, CA: Hermagoras Press).
10 Robert Scholes, *The Rise and Fall of English: Reconstructing English as a Discipline* (New Haven, CT: Yale University Press, 1998), 10-11.
11 Janet Emig, *The Composing Process of Twelfth Graders* (Champaign, IL: National Council of Teachers of English, 1971).
12 Richard Young, "Paradigms and Problems: Needed Research in Rhetorical Invention," in *Research in Composing*, ed. C. Cooper and L. Odell (Urbana, IL: National Council of English Teachers, 1978).
13 Janet Emig interview with Julie Jensen, "Broad Shoulders and Big Issues: Council Leaders Tell Their Stories," *English Journal* 89, no. 3 (2000): 100.
14 Hairston, "The Winds of Change."
15 Scholes, *The Rise and Fall of English*, 6-7.
16 Noreen Garman and Maria Piantanida, "The Academic/Professional Portfolio," *The Australian Administrator* 12, no. 3 (1991): 3.
17 Judith Arter and Vicki Spandel, "Using Portfolios of Student Work in Instruction and Assessment," *Educational Measurement: Issues and Practice* (Spring 1992).
18 Richard Wilbur, "Advice to a Prophet," in *The Poems of Richard Wilbur* (New York: Harcourt Brace Jovanovich, 1963), 6.
19 Hairston, "The Winds of Change," and James Berlin and Robert Inkster, "Current Traditional Rhetoric: Paradigm and Practice," in *Freshman English News* (Winter 1980).
20 Sondra Perl in "Understanding Composition" in *Landmark Essays on the Writing Process*, says that in recursive writing, "There is a forward-moving action that exists by a backward-moving action. Most writers reread bits of discourse already on the page. They also return to some key word or item, she says, when stuck. Lastly, there is a felt sense in authors which involves non-verbalized perceptions that surround the words and evoke something in the writer. The felt sense calls forth images and ideas in the writer so that the writing process is not just linear nor just from the mind.
21 Here my student echoes Heilbrun, *Writing a Woman's Life* and Emig, *The Composing Process of Twelfth Graders*.
22 Berlin and Inkster, "Current Traditional Rhetoric."
23 Thomas Schwandt, "On Understanding Understanding," *Qualitative Inquiry* 5, no. 4 (1999): 453.
24 Peter Elbow, "What Do We Mean When We Talk about Voice in Texts?" in *Voices on Voice: Perspectives, Definitions, Inquiry*, ed. K. Yancy (United States of America: National Council of Teachers of English, 1994), 19.
25 Adrienne Rich, "Claiming an Education," *in On Lies, Secrets, and Silence: Selected Prose 1966-1978* (New York: W.W. Norton & Company, 1979).

26 Paulo Freire, *Pedagogy of the Oppressed*, trans. M.B. Ramos (New York: Herder and Herder, 1970).
27 Nicholas Burbules, "A Theory of Power in Education," *Educational Theory* 36, no. 2 (1986).

Essay Five

The Crucible: Authority and The Matter of Time

In a corner of my classroom a print titled "The Alchemist" rests on top of a filing cabinet. I've always been drawn to this picture of a medieval scientist. His laboratory space, crammed with earthenware pots, bottles and books, also contains a kiln, on top of it is a crucible or a vessel for the molten metal burned while seeking gold. The scientist fans a small fire as craftsmen at a nearby table busy themselves with other matters. Quaint-looking containers cover tables and intense activity is suggested in this room crowded with artifacts of a science now thought to have been searching for the impossible. The preoccupied and intent look on the face of the scientist garbed in a loosely fitted gown contrasts with the story the painting suggests about the world around him. A small cat watches a mouse and a curious spectator peers in a window. Meanwhile, outside of the lab, I imagine that people gather in a market and go about their business unconcerned and unaware of the "matter" of the alchemist.

The work of the alchemist intrigues me, that desire to transform leaden matter into gold. Yet, how easy it is, as Berman notes, to regard the "thinking of previous ages not simply as other legitimate forms of consciousness, but as misguided world views that we have happily outgrown."[1] Lacking a medieval consciousness and possessing centuries of intellectual heritage, how dismissive we can be. But even a failed endeavor may call forth new understandings; in fact may be essential to new understandings. This is why the notion of alchemy appeals to me as an overarching metaphor for these essays. If I take a metaphorical view of alchemy and its belief that "all metals are in the process of becoming gold,"[2] I may view even the failure of transforming a pedagogy as forming a more expansive consciousness. It makes sense then for me to use alchemy, along with a crucible metaphor, as a framing device for the second part of this study of a pedagogy of authority.

In the essays that follow, episodes recorded in my teaching journals allow me to hold my new student-centered and feminist practices up to the light of my former pedagogy. Journal writings record how I desire to alter my "leaden" state. Yet they also reveal that I am unwilling to be refined in the crucible, so I swing wildly between blaming students or blaming myself for "failure" of my newly constructed pedagogy. More brittle of ego than malleable, I lock myself into the suppositions of an either/or consciousness and suffer the consequences of this way of thinking.

In each essay I examine one aspect or "matter" of pedagogy. The raw "matter," if you will, comes from student writings, conversations, and teaching journals that I then re-visit through this writing. In this essay, "The Crucible: Authority and the Matter of Time," I speculate on authority in a temporal sense and characterize traditional pedagogy as fettered by time. I then juxtapose traditional educational practices against a pedagogical approach to process writing when I attempt to undo time's tyranny. This discussion is situated against a backdrop of profound personal loss and a grief unending.

Each episode within "A Matter of Time" contains an "excess" or what Fiske calls "overflowing semiosis" where "excess" meaning escapes ideological control.[3] In a traditional approach to pedagogy, my language supplies the excess as I by-pass a rightful enactment of authority and move into the authoritarian. A second example, cast within a student-centered approach, also contains an excess. This essay portrays what happens when my pedagogy creates an "excess" of "personal" or student time, when I "give" my authority to students.

In the subsequent essay, "The Crucible: Authority and the Matter of Texts," I speculate on textual interpretation and talk about how locating authority either within the text or within the reader alters not only content of the discipline, but the authority of the teacher. Episodes from my teaching journals reveal either/or framing of classroom events, events that hold an excess of symbol in what I name "Back behind the Podium." Only later, through the writing of this study, do I come to realize that "pedagogy is a much messier and more inconclusive affair than the vast majority of educational theories and practices make it out to be.[4]

DEAD-LINES

Like a zealot, I tore through my new room, dragging desks from evenly spaced rows to make circles, hanging a Famous Women poster alongside *Miss Saigon*, *The Fantastiks*, *Sunset Boulevard*, and *Hamlet*. I relegated the podium to a corner outside the circle where it stood "like a stone savage unarmed" as Frost says in "Mending Wall," behind a wall of desks three deep. (I should have asked then what I thought I was walling in and walling out as Frost does in his poem. But I believed I knew, kept telling myself everything "felt right.")

So I began. In my room. It was 1995. I would overthrow, overturn, topple as many of my past teaching practices as possible. At least that was my intention. The decision was a conscious one. I would begin in earnest to enact a different pedagogy, a pedagogy based on "constructed knowledge." Avoiding lectures and "the standard peacock model" of pedagogy intended to "dazzle the hens" as Miller says,[5] I no longer wanted my knowledge or my "self" to be the centerpiece of the classroom. With my newly shaped feminist and constructivist understandings, I would "open" dialogue, make a space where the subjective knowledge of students mattered, where their experiences became the text of the classroom, where they "gave voice" to their stories and their interpretations of texts. In short, the experiential and personal (sometimes even my personal) would be the text and "matter" of the classroom. In this conception of pedagogy, students would claim their education,[6] take responsibility for their learning, be involved. The discussion circle symbolized this for me, symbolized my desire for shared understandings, shared authority. No longer would I perform a role of the authoritarian and traditional teacher, the one who made pronouncements, who dropped esoteric tidbits intended to impress, who "popped quizzes," who initiated "sneak attacks" to keep students off balance or "properly neurotic" (the "proper state" for students, I used to tell them).

"Now that I think about it," I wrote in my journal on August 24, 1995, "last year I planned due dates with students, asking that they tell me about conflicts with other papers or dates to be avoided." Considering student schedules first was not typical of me; in the past, I announced a due date—period—a "No late" policy enforced. Either I received a paper on time, I told them, or it didn't exist. Either/or thinking my *modus operandi*.

I remember how I joked that the due date for the paper was the Dead-line. "Think about *that* metaphor," I would say with a metaphorical wink: "**DEAD**-line." Now I, an English teacher of twenty-five years, was asking students to help set due dates; this from the teacher who repeatedly told students to get assigned papers to the school on time, "Unless you have a date with a mortician." (This one always requiring some heavy emphasis.)

As I look back now, I see more than a desire to overturn teaching method or epistemology. I felt a personal desire to unmask myself. Loss can do that—make you shed trappings that weigh you down, that sap energy because it takes so much effort to keep up the appearance of things. In the previous five years I had experienced two deaths—the death of my mother, which brought with it a grief unending; and the closing of St. Mary, which brought a grief that I later resolved by overturning many inherited ideas that I learned there. Loss had taught me that when death stakes its claim, the "matter" of life changes—what really matters, I mean.

Thrown back on myself, I began a process of self-reflection that is still on-going. (The memoir, *A Life in School: What the Teacher Learned* by Jane Tompkins,[7] helped me understand this.) That one loss followed so soon after the other gave introspection a kind of womb-like quietude and a space to re-assemble myself. "We think back through our mothers if we are women," Rich tells us.[8] I now realize how this thinking may happen.

In my present reading of the "DEAD-line" narrative, I'm struck by the way I enacted authority. Embedded in the jokes, tropes and pronouncements, I see a teacher who exceeds rightful authority. Rightful authority expects compliance and obedience,[9] but my tropes of intimidation, subtle and perhaps even playful, were aggressively defensive, enacted *to* instill fear and enacted *from* fear. In being purposefully ambiguous through the language of metaphor, I avoided the literal and manipulated the figurative in a way that amplified my authority, pushed it into the authoritarian by soaking my language with menace.

I'm reminded of an article I read in *Writers* magazine advising fictionalists to "humanize" evil characters. Remember Hannibal Lechter in the film *Silence of the Lambs*? He was a sociopath and a cannibal who became utterly and chillingly believable because his persona *was not* evil incarnate. Characterized as soft spoken, genteel and sophisticated, his civility lured the unsuspecting for his cannibalism. But this very civility made him more seductive and believable, adding texture to his character, a texture making interpretation of him more troubling, more problematic. In a similar way, by masking my authoritarian practices under a veneer of humor and metaphor, I strained the traditional discourse of schooling to portray something more than what was a rightful enactment of authority. It was an excess. Fiske talks about the idea of excessiveness as meaning out of control, meaning that exceeds the norms of ideological control or the requirements of any specific text." He then adds, "Excess is overflowing semiosis, the excessive sign performs the work of the dominant ideology, but then exceeds and overspills it, leaving excess meaning that escapes ideological control and is free to be used to resist or evade it."[10]

MOVABLE DUE DATES

"Ms. Logsdon," Effie said pleasantly, "You're a wimp."

Only after hearing her voice did I realize her presence in my classroom. Engaged in an intense conversation with Ann, a junior having problems with her research paper, I had failed to see Effie. I was suggesting that Ann get some additional critical sources and that perhaps a rethinking of one of her thesis points would be necessary. Then, I moved her deadline.

It was not unusual for me to grant extensions if a student expressed a need for more time. I granted extensions freely. (This another practice of my "new" pedagogy.) Sometimes I suggested a re-conceptualization of a particular idea. Sometimes I suggested another re-write of a first draft. Sometimes a student said she needed more time because of personal troubles. But, whatever the case, moving a due date did not trouble me. (Not until I realized the repercussions of my actions.)

But here was Effie, smiling and gently chiding me. I turned toward the voice and said, "Why is that, Effie. Why am I a wimp? Because I gave Ann that extension?" After pausing briefly, I added, "Are you upset because you already turned in your paper?"

Just then, another English teacher joined us. "No, that isn't it," Effie claimed. "It's just that they're procrastinating and you let them." After my colleague asked what was going on, he chimed in, "Not like me, huh, Effie? I don't give extensions, do I?" Effie quickly assented, and I turned to Jim, and said, "Oh, I get it. I'm a wimp if I give an extension even if I grant one because a student needs time to work on an idea or improve her writing so she will have a better paper. This makes me a wimp, right?"

"That's right," Jim said matter of factly. Effie's smile told me she agreed.

But I was not content to let the matter drop. "So if I enforce deadlines," I said in a measured tone, "make everyone turn in her paper on time no matter what troubles she might be having, then that's good and that makes me a good teacher, too. Right?" I never got a response though because other students entered the room just then.

So my question hung there in its rhetorical space, suspending our conversation.

What to make of the "wimp" comment? What to make of it now that the tincture of time has softened its sting?

Watching this conversation unfold again as I write it, I realize now that I had been thinking about deadlines, ideas of good teacher/ bad teacher, concepts of knowledge and pedagogy. I am the one who brings up the "good teacher" in this episode because I had been sensing that other students felt as Effie did.

But it is apparent that the "Ms. Logsdon, you're a wimp" pedagogy represents an opposite practice of the "DEAD-line" pedagogy. I had been coming to change for a few years, as I've explained. But once I tried on a few new things one year—portfolios and narrative writing especially—I committed myself to change in the following year, a move that in many ways was North/South or thesis/antithesis.

So even as I recognize that Effie's comment may have meant that some students took advantage of my more humane impulses, there is still an idea embedded in the wimp comment that conflates time and its mastery with knowledge and with ideas of "good" teaching and authority.

These are ideas easily recognized once we take them out to look at them. Laidlaw and Sumara say schooling is rooted in Cartesian ideas about time. They remember how "clock time dominated" their student experience and catalog the following:

TIMETABLES. BELLS. "SCOPE AND SEQUENCE"
CURRICULUM DOCUMENTS. DAY PLANS WHICH MUST
"ACCOUNT" FOR EVERY MINUTE; YEARLY OVERVIEWS

WHERE TIME AND EVENTS TRAVEL ALONG A "TIME LINE," WITH SKILLS TO BE MASTERED AT SCHEDULED INTERVALS, AND DATES OF COMPLETION AND ACHIEVEMENT ALREADY DETERMINED."[11]

But time is more than a mere scaffold of learning. Think about the ways we measure knowledge by credit hour, by semester, "mastery" by assessment and grade point averages, how we "keep up" or "fall behind" last year by marking our place in the textbook or by counting the number of papers we correct. If time were merely a scaffold, we would only note it in how we parcel the school day into periods, use bells to mark beginnings and endings, signify openings from closings.

It seems to me that ever since we learned how to measure days with mechanized timepieces, with clocks that struck or sounded the hour, we've supposed that we, and not just our inventions, have "mastered" time. We've lived beyond the time when light, dark and seasons marked the experiences and labors of our lives. As Boorstin notes, the first instruments measured time by sun and shadow, through flowing sand or water—visual images.[12] But once inventors figured out how to pound metal on metal to gauge the hour, natural things, like the sun and sand, were no longer needed. Time, in effect, became an "object," and mechanical timepieces, ironically, yet another way to master nature. (Think how thick are our metaphors about time—we lose it, waste it, save it, spend it, Latinize it—*Tempus Fuget, Carpe diem*.)

So now, when I reconsider Effie's comment, I see myself as a teacher who enacted a pedagogy where writing and thinking required both space and time to evolve. Even though I set a due date for collecting research papers, I had come to reject the notion that a predetermined time worked for everyone in the same way. I saw the lesson I intended to teach as the recursive nature of writing and thinking, or process writing. I thought that I honored unique individuals not some abstract idea of "student" or a universally imposed notion of time with its attendant idea that a significant part of learning was to "master" content within a specified time. I allowed time to unravel; I expanded it.

But to Effie, I was a wimp. I allowed students who procrastinated "extra" time. (The irony in "extending" time is not lost on me, nor the issue of control implied here by my being the one to extend it.) In enacting a student-centered pedagogy, I focused on student needs, student time. To Effie's way of thinking (and mine in the DEAD-line) by not punishing students who failed to meet deadlines, I no longer "mastered" time, nor did I expect my students to master it. In doing this, I weakened my authority. I didn't demand that students turn in papers by a certain day. (I never again mentioned the mortician.) I didn't punish behavior that failed to show a mastery of time. The student determined when her writing and revision had refined her ideas. Thus, she authored her writing and authorized the "time" of her learning.

So, while drawing a rather romanticized view of this student-centered process approach to pedagogy, difficulties remained. I want to point out these troubles now; show where the rosy picture greys; offer some of my more recent thoughts about "excess" and the matter of time within a pedagogy of authority.

Educational practices, according to Ellsworth, like research, writing, and pedagogy, are representational practices that try to "control excessive moments in education through research protocols, proper forms of academic writing, and curricular norms and standards."[13] In going against traditional notions of time and the role of the teacher as the timekeeper (the one who determines how much time is needed for the mastery of a particular knowledge), the "wimp" episode draws a portrait of excess.

In this "wimp" story, I created an "excess" of time. Movable deadlines removed the usual teacher authority of prescribing specific guidelines for the completion of assignments, leaving students to their own devices. Without the usual academic requirements and markers, this excess of time gave some students the opportunity to avoid thinking and writing until the last minute (the end of the semester). Doing this threw them right back into the kind of writing practice I was trying to transform. In other words, students who procrastinated lost the opportunity to learn writing as process. I, in turn, lost the opportunity to mentor their writing, to reside within the writing process as audience and author. Thus, the recursive nature of the pedagogy was lost. This then undermined my authority as an expert within the pedagogy of process writing (for those students).

For students like Effie, I weakened the authority attached not only to disciplining practices, but to knowledge. (How the disciplines we teach, discipline in multiple ways.) "Good" teachers demand assignments on time, assign deadlines, ensure that students obey and are held accountable. Good teachers in traditional pedagogy parcel out time because their "expert" authority "predicts" or "controls" the amount of time students will need to "master" knowledge. Good teachers assert their authority by commanding obedience. Movable deadlines made me a "wimp," weak, ineffectual, without authority.

By practicing a pedagogy of excess time, I also sacrificed myself on a rack of educational realities particularly known to English teachers. Because I permitted students more time to write, I constrained the amount of time I had to correct. Deadlines given to me by the institutions were not movable. As Walkerdine says of the progressive educator, I became like the nurturing mother who sacrifices everything for the child whose needs must be met at all times. In progressive education, there is a cost to liberation, she says, but the cost is borne by the teacher, as it is borne by the mother.[14] Steedman suggests that this role mirrors "not the aristocratic mother, but the paid servant of the aristocracy, who is always there to service the children."[15]

But representational practices follow two laws, as Phelan notes. She says that a representation, like a pedagogy, always "conveys more than it intends; and it is never totalizing." She theorizes that "The excess meaning conveyed by representation creates a supplement that makes multiple and resistant readings possible." Phelan also claims that "because of representation's supplemental excess and its failure to be totalizing, close readings of the logic of representation can produce psychic resistance and, possibly, political change.[16]

In light of these theories, I now come to understand that I would never have gotten to the "Ms. Logsdon, you're a wimp" episode had it not been for my excesses in the DEAD-line episode. As an authoritarian, I created a supplement to educational discourse that also produced a rupture within that discourse. After coming to a place where I experienced dissonance with traditional pedagogy, I moved to new practices that I believed overturned past practices with their lockstep linearity and deadlines. I abandoned the excessive language of authority, language which had spilled its excess into authoritarian practices. I no longer lashed students with a pedagogy overly-determined on obedience. I no longer subscribed to practices based on ideas that thought "to be disciplined was to do someone else's work in someone else's frame to meet someone else's deadline."[17] These pedagogical practices of authority became apparent to me when I began new teaching practices.

Later, as I examined the "Ms. Logsdon, you're a wimp" episode, I came to see other excesses. Here I allowed an over-determination of student authority that intervened and even subverted the very pedagogy I sought to enact. In attempting to level the hierarchy that legitimately positioned me as authority within the institution, I sought an egalitarian authority."[18] I realize, now, I found not a pedagogy of authority but a pedagogy of impossibility. In enacting a pedagogy that emphasized student needs to the exclusion of my pedagogical needs as a teacher, I diminished the pedagogical relationship which is, in part, founded on epistemic authority.

I am coming to view the pedagogical relationship between teacher and student as one where the matter of time needs to be negotiated. There will always be competing interests within the pedagogical relationship of authority that are unresolvable. But thinking that authority resides within one person or another denies that authority itself is a relationship. "Giving" authority to either one or the other in the relationship creates an excess that proves to be destructive to pedagogy and to the people in the relationship. Now I realize that if I move into a more expansive consciousness and avoid either/or constructions of authority that either place authority with me as teacher or with the student, I may view my pedagogy as *constructing time* instead of thinking that time constructs my pedagogy. If I can do this, I may avoid future authoritarian excesses, the stress I felt from absorbing the relative and movable deadlines, the hurt I felt with Effie's comment.

If I view my pedagogy, like this writing, as never really finished but continually evolving, as a co-constructed space between student and teacher where struggle is inevitable, then I may avoid the imperative of either/or thinking. As Sommers suggestions:

> THESE EITHER/OR WAYS OF SEEING EXCLUDE LIFE AND REAL REVISION BY PUSHING US TO SAFE POSITIONS, TO WHAT IS KNOWN. THEY ARE SAFE POSITIONS THAT EXCLUDE EACH OTHER AND DON'T ALLOW FOR ANY AMBIGUITY, UNCERTAINTY. ONLY WHEN I SUSPEND MYSELF BETWEEN EITHER AND OR CAN I MOVE AWAY FROM CONVENTIONAL BOUNDARIES AND BEGIN TO SEE SHAPES AND CONTOURS— AMBIGUITY, AND DISCONTINUITY, MOMENTS WHEN THE SEAMS OF LIFE JUST DON'T WANT TO HOLD. . ."[19]

If I view the excesses in my pedagogy like the metals of alchemy that must be heated so they expand, be turned into liquid so they may be distilled, then I may be able to alter a consciousness through the crucible that is my classroom. Then I may, as Atkins suggests, "break out of the pernicious trap of binary-oppositional thinking, which is ineluctably hierarchical and maintained by violence in which self is always engaged in fierce competition with other."[20] It is a consciousness that admittedly can never be fully aware of itself,[21] but a consciousness that may be expanded and made more aware of itself through writing. It is a consciousness resembling the one sought by the medieval alchemist.

The consciousness of the medieval according to Berman accepted that reality is paradoxical, that things and their opposites are closely related. Seeing the connections in disparate matter, alters thinking, alters pedagogy. The rejection of alchemy, according to Jung coincided with the repression of the unconscious, a characteristic of the West since the Scientific Revolution.[22] Jung believed that the failure of each individual to confront personal demons, that part of the personality to be hated and feared, inevitably had disastrous consequences. Alchemy then was not merely a scientific exercise; it was a psychic journey that attempted to re-introduce the unconscious into the conscious mind. This is what writing has enable me to do—attempt to surface the unconscious, take a psychic journey, name my demons and name desires.

Thus, fear of "losing" authority constructed one pedagogy and the fear of "losing" learning constructed the other. A pedagogy of authority recognizes mutuality and agency of both teacher and student, works on the assumption that no one holds or possesses authority, therefore fear of losing it is founded on obdurate rock of illusion on which all pedagogies falter. A pedagogy of authority then works through the idea that "the pedagogical relationship between student and teacher is a paradox. . .that poses problems that can never be settled or resolved once and for all."[23]

Notes

1   Morris Berman, *The Reenchantment of the World* (Ithaca, NY: Cornell University Press, 1981), 70.
2   Ibid., 88.
3   John Fiske, *Understanding Popular Culture* (London: Routledge, 1991).
4   Elizabeth Ellsworth, *Teaching Positions: Difference, Pedagogy, and the Power of Address* (New York: Teachers College Press, 1997), 8.
5   Nancy K. Miller, "Mastery, Identity, and the Politics of Work: A Feminist Teacher in the Graduate School Classroom," in *Gendered Subjects: The Dynamics of Feminist Teaching*, ed. M. Culley and C. Portuges (Bost: Routledge, 1985), 198.
6   Adrienne Rich, "Claiming an Education," in *On Lies, Secrets, and Silence: Selected Prose 1966-1978* (New York: W.W. Norton & Company, 1979).
7   Jane Thompkins, *A Life in School: What the Teacher Learned* (New York: Addison-Wesley Publishing, Inc., 1996).
8   Adrienne Rich, "On Claiming an Education."

9   E.D. Watt, *Authority* (New York: St. Martin's Press, 1982).
10 Fiske, *Understanding Popular Culture*, 114.
11 Linda Laidlaw and Dennis Sumara, "Transforming Pedagogical Time," *Journal of Curriculum Theorizing* 16, no. 1 (2000): 11.
12 Daniel Boorstin, *The Discoverers* (New York: Vintage Books, 1983).
13 Ellsworth, *Teaching Positions*, 72.
14 Valerie Walkerdine, "Progressive Pedagogy and Political Struggle," in *Feminism and Critical Pedagogy*, ed. C. Luke and J. Gore (New York: Routledge, 1992).
15 Steedman cited in Walkerdine, "Progressive Pedagogy and Political Struggle," 21.
16 Peggy Phelan, *Unmarked: The Politics of Performance* (New York: Routledge, 1993), 3.
17 Deborah a. Dooley, *Plain and Ordinary Things* (Albany: State University of New York Press, 1995), 118.
18 Watt, *Authority*.
19 Nancy Sommers, "Between the Drafts," in *Women/Writing/Teaching*, ed. J.Z. Schmidt (Albany: State University of New York Press, 1998), 18.
20 G. Douglas Atkins, "Introduction: Literary Theory, Critical Practice, and the Classroom," in *Contemporary Literary Theory*, ed. G.D. Atkins and L. Morrow (Amherst: The University of Massachusetts Press, 1989), 18.
21 Soshana Felman, "Psychoanalysis and Education: Teaching the Terminable and Interminable," *Yale French Studies* no. 63 (June 7, 1982).
22 Berman, *The Reenchantment of the World*.
23 Ellsworth, *Teaching Positions*, 8.

Essay Six

The Crucible: Authority and the Matter of Texts

Even before I became a literature teacher, I held texts in a kind of awe. This reverence came from a love of literature which I believed led me to reflect on the "fundamental questions of human existence—what it meant to be a person, to engage in significant relationship with others, to live from the vital centre of the most essential values."[1] Thus, literature for me was art and more; it offered "the possibility of meaningfulness."[2]

But my awe formed before I realized that the criteria of what counted as literature was ideological,[3] that literary "authorities" heard some "voices," were deaf to others; embraced some cultures and neglected others; valued some authors and dismissed others, often on the basis of gender, race, or other social category. When I recognized what was excluded from the literature that "counted" (women much like myself), my awe diminished, and I came to see that works of literature are culturally scripted.

When I accepted the belief that "anything that carries meaning" can be a text,[4] I changed other views as well. I acknowledged the relationship between the reader and the text as central, a change that caused me to accept the reader's experience of the text as significant for meaning making.[5] This meant that I no longer assumed the text to be the final arbitrator of meaning, as preached by New Criticism, the theory I had learned and practiced. In rejecting the positivist idea that a text is an "autonomous object"[6] with determinate and stable meaning located *within* it, I also rejected my former beliefs that privilege text over reader, beliefs that suggest "that standards [of interpretation] are concrete and objective rather than subjective and relativistic."[7] In other words, I moved toward a reader-response orientation that gives the reader, and the reading community, the authority over meaning and claims that texts are situated and meanings socially constructed.

With a re-formed theory of texts, I now have a deeper understanding of the word "text" in terms of its Latin root: *texere*, "to weave" and "to join or fit together," and *textum*, "to plait, braid, interweave, interlace; to construct."[8] Thus, a text, "that which is woven, a web," suggests, as poststructuralists insist, that there is no single truth or meaning in a text; "there is no 'end' to interpretation, no limit to ways texts can be read, and therefore no 'end' to the meanings of a text."[9] (And, as Derrida maintains, no author of a text either.[10])

Thus, all literary texts are woven from other literary texts, and in a more radical sense "every word, phrase, or segment is a reworking of other writings which precede or surround the individual work."[11] In more recent extensions of the word "text," semiotic and deconstructive writers use the word to refer to "the fabric of culture itself, in which we and our students find ourselves already woven, even as we try to learn and teach how to weave or reweave those garments."[12]

With this brief discussion as backdrop, I consider Authority and the Matter of Texts in this essay. Here I talk about my evolving pedagogy in light of a story about texts. I portray how a changing view of knowledge alters how I view texts, readers, literary canons, interpretations, and authority. Yet, even as I struggle to enact a pedagogy that reflects my thinking, troubles keep occurring. These troubles play out in my classroom, the crucible where the matter of texts and my pedagogy are tempered.

I use an episode from my teaching journal, "Back Behind the Podium" and "read through" an implication that psychoanalysis has for pedagogy. To "read through" according to Ellsworth is not a way of citing an authority, or establishing a point, or borrowing an apt use of language. Nor does reading through use other texts as static, given, or known filters for each other. To Ellsworth, reading through is a way of giving "a different sensibility" to the questions she asks. It is a way of holding different texts next to each other so that one illuminates the other. Thus, reading through "highlights the *process* of my reading and draws attention to the interest I bring to reading and to how those interests shape the meanings I construct."[13]

Thus, two processes combine here to illuminate possible meanings in student responses to my pedagogy and my responses to them—reading and writing. Through these processes I portray how I am locked in either/or thinking about authority and texts, blaming students or blaming myself for dissonance I feel. Journal writings and conversations portray my struggle to temper my "self" as I grapple with authority, texts, and pedagogy and continue to move to a more expansive consciousness.

BACK BEHIND THE PODIUM

"Where is all of this going?" Gina asked.

"Where is all of this going?" I repeated to myself. "What does she mean?"

I felt caught. Thrown. I tried to gather myself even though panic made my throat dry. She had challenged the way I was allowing the discussion to unfold, I thought, and this a mere two weeks into the school year. We were having a rather random conversation about the novel, *Equus*. Then I asked a question about religious practices of self-abuse. After several students volunteered responses, Gina made her demand.

I didn't show any sign of affront and made a rather perfunctory comment, but I was not satisfied with my response. From the look on Gina's face, I saw that she wasn't satisfied either. But, I really couldn't think clearly because I really didn't know where the discussion was going.

The day after this incident, I sounded the alarums, as Shakespeare would say, and pulled my new pedagogy of texts into retreat. My journal records what happened next:

> SOMETIMES I AMAZE MYSELF WITH HOW SENSITIVE I AM TO CLASS DISCUSSION AND MY OWN VULNERABILITIES. REGARDING THE GINA INCIDENT. THE NEXT DAY SHE WAS QUITE DIFFERENT AND SO WAS I. SHE SEEMED TO BE UNCERTAIN AND NOT AT ALL EXPECTING/DEMANDING "WHERE'S ALL OF THIS GOING?" NOW I WAS TAKING CHARGE—*BACK BEHIND MY PODIUM* AND STANDING, NOT SITTING AMONG THE STUDENTS.
>
> DISCUSSION WENT WELL. I HAD A LOT TO SAY ABOUT DIFFERENT TYPES OF CRITICISM (MARXIST, FEMINIST) AND HOW CERTAIN VIEWS COLOR INTERPRETATIONS OR ARE USED AS A LENS TO READ LITERATURE. ALL OF THIS CAME ABOUT IN RESPONSE TO A QUESTION A STUDENT ASKED—NOT PART OF A PLANNED LECTURE. STILL I FELT MUCH BETTER ABOUT WHAT I WAS SAYING. STUDENTS DIDN'T ASK TOO MANY QUESTIONS AND I KNEW THEY WOULDN'T. I WAS ASSURED, UNASSAILABLE, AND KNEW IT. IS THIS WHAT GAVE ME CONFIDENCE—KNOWING THAT THEY COULD NOT MATCH ME? I WAS THE EXPERT AND THEY WERE THE STUDENTS. HOW DO I FEEL ABOUT THIS? TODAY, MORE REASSURED. MORE COMFORTABLE IN CLASS. BACK ON KEEL.
>
> "WHERE IS ALL OF THIS GOING?"

Gina's question had provoked in me a need to gather more forces (perhaps battalions) of textual authority because she had attacked where I was most vulnerable. As I look back at this episode now, I read it in terms of what it says to me about texts, knowledge, pedagogy, and resistance.

I believe that Gina, in trying to make pedagogical sense out of my lesson, expressed a desire to connect textual analysis to an eventual meaning "in" the text. In this way of thinking (based on New Criticism), close reading, attentiveness to language, symbol, and image systematically combine as "methods" that insure a "final" explication (mastery). I interpreted Gina's question to mean that I, the authority, the dispenser of interpretations that mattered, was responsible for leading discussion to a "final" and "correct" analysis. (I knew this approach well. I, too, had grown up with it.) But my new approach to texts failed to follow this strategy.

I think also that Gina desired a transmission of textual knowledge of the kind that Freire[14] talks about as a "banking" concept in *Pedagogy of the Oppressed*. Here, there is a flow of knowledge from the authority, the master, the one who is supposed to know, to the one who needs to know, the apprentice. In this pedagogy, educating then becomes "an act of depositing," where students become the "receptacles" to be "filled" with deposits from the teacher. Students then learn to duplicate texts that the teacher presents as knowledge in a one way process destined to replicate and not transform.

As I now read the text Gina presented to me through her question, I see a student who expected a knowledge "aimed at its ideal: the exhaustion—through methodical investigation—of all there is to know; the absolute completion—termination—of apprenticeship."[15] New Criticism makes this kind of assumption about knowledge in approaching meaning as the end or final result of applying painstakingly thorough methods of analysis to a text. If a reader "applies" the "correct" technique, a work of art yields its meaning. Thus, as an apprentice to *my* learning and *my* instruction, I believe that Gina desired textual knowledge that terminated in mastery—a mastery of the knowledge I passed on to her, a mastery of the text, and thus a mastery of meaning. Because my lesson failed to lead to these ends, Gina would remain an apprentice, "ignorant."

This then is how I interpreted the text that Gina presented to me in her question, "Where is all of this going?" But the episode reveals my position also. So I now offer a reading of where I was in this matter of texts, pedagogy, knowledge, and resistance.

My journal records that on the day following Gina's comment I went back behind the podium. Taking "charge." Enacting the role of teacher as authority, master. (Lacan notes how even our academic degrees express the idea that knowledge is finite and knowable—Master of Arts.[16]) Putting on a role scripts a text that students read and then interpret. My position "back behind the podium" carried with it an image of one who is supposed to know. The role *itself* presented me "with" a knowing and "as" knowing—"with" a knowledge (the role) that is certain, contained, defined, and determined, and "as" knowing (the knowledge the authority presents).

In other words, when I "performed" a role from behind the podium, the text of my teacher performance called forth predetermined responses, interpretations that could be read and then reproduced ritually each time enacted. Performing an authoritarian text as I did offers knowledge that *seems* complete, absolute, certain. However, this performance of the role and the type of knowledge it presents, re-presents a knowledge (seemingly) in possession of itself and able to know itself.[17] It denies the unpredictable with the pedagogical act and denies the role of the unconscious. But there is another way to view this episode in relation to knowledge and the unconscious, a way of thinking new to me, but a way I take up here, even as I write, so that I may come to understand in a deeper way.

I now read through this matter of texts with Felman's theory of the "implication of psychoanalysis in pedagogy." Felman comes to her theory through the texts of Lacan and before him, Freud. Basically she claims that psychoanalysis has shifted pedagogy because of the unconscious, the "knowledge that does not know itself." Accepting the notion of an unconscious then denies the possibility of absolute knowledge and "displaces our very modes of intelligibility." It is the unconscious, a kind of *unmeant knowledge* that makes "human knowledge, by definition, that which is *untotalizable*, that which rules out any possibility of totalizing what it knows or of eradicating its own ignorance."[18]

Felman offers the following theory that I summarizes here.[19] She says that if one accepts Lacan's idea that "The discovery of the unconscious . . . is that the implications of meaning infinitely exceed the signs manipulated by the individual," then we mobilize many more signs (through speaking in "slips" or dreams) than we can ever *know*."[20] If this is so, then "there can constitutively be no such thing as absolute knowledge; absolute knowledge is knowledge that has exhausted its own articulation."[21]

Yet, Felman adds, "articulated knowledge is by definition what cannot exhaust its own self-knowledge." What follows is that for "knowledge to be spoken, linguistically articulated, it would constitutively have to be supported by the ignorance carried by language, the ignorance of the *excess of signs* that of necessity its language—its articulation—"mobilizes."[22] Thus, human knowledge is by definition untotalizable.

Felman claims that this epistemological principle "of the irreducibility of ignorance which stems from the unconscious, receives confirmation from modern science." She mentions mathematics and set theory of Cantor, that "the set of all sets in a universe does not constitute a set."[23] She also cites the "uncertainty principle" of Heisenberg in physics.

From here, Felman then claims that ignorance is "no longer simply *opposed* to knowledge: it is itself a radical condition, an integral part of the very structure of knowledge." So, teaching then, like analysis, has to deal "not so much with lack of knowledge as the *resistances* to knowledge," a desire to ignore that is "less cognitive than performative."[24] Freud also commented on the relationship between ignorance and resistance:

> IT IS A LONG SUPERSEDED IDEA. . . THAT THE PATIENT SUFFERS FROM A SORT OF IGNORANCE AND THAT IF ONE REMOVES THIS IGNORANCE BY GIVING HIM INFORMATION [ABOUT THE CAUSAL CONNECTION OF HIS ILLNESS WITH HIS LIFE, ABOUT HIS EXPERIENCES IN CHILDHOOD, AND SO ON] HE IS BOUND TO RECOVER. THE PATHOLOGICAL FACTOR IS NOT HIS IGNORANCE IN ITSELF, BUT THE ROOT OF THIS IGNORANCE IS HIS *INNER RESISTANCES*. IT IS THEY WHO

FIRST CALLED THIS IGNORANCE INTO BEING, AND THEY STILL MAINTAIN IT NOW. THE TASK OF THE TREATMENT LIES IN COMBATING THESE RESISTANCES.[25]

While I am aware that many modern critiques have rejected some of Freud's theories and I do not claim to be a Freudian scholar, there are aspects of what he says that may be applied to pedagogy. I resonate with these ideas about resistance to knowledge. One new pedagogical lesson that psychoanalysis offers pedagogy according to Felman is that ignorance itself may teach us something and become itself instructive.[26] The lesson comes from Freud through Lacan and it says that we need "to interpret the phenomenon of doubt as an integral part of the message."[27] If we do this, the pedagogical questions become: Where is the ignorance—the resistance to knowledge—located? How can I interpret out of the dynamic ignorance I analytically encounter, both in others and in myself?[28]

Holding Felman's text[29] alongside the text of "Back behind the podium" enables me to read in it signs of my resistance. I now read "Where is this all going?" as a text that shows resistance to a new enactment of a pedagogy of authority. In retreating to a comfortable and known place—behind the podium—I resisted a new construct of authority that would have positioned me as merely another interpreter of texts, rather than the one who possessed sole authority over meaning.

Because I perceived a reader-response pedagogy as an "anything goes" approach to texts, I allowed discussion to unravel with no tie to a pedagogical purpose. Then, when confronted with my own confusion over what I perceived as a "loss" of both textual authority and pedagogical authority, I avoided thinking through the implications of the situation and retreated instead to an enactment of authority that relied on a role. Fear drove me to re-present myself in a role of authority as the one who has mastery over the knowledge she dispenses. Unwilling to see that pedagogy is a far "messier" business than is supposed, I denied what Ellsworth calls the "paradox of pedagogy"—that a teacher's performance is a "necessarily suspended or authorless performance," whereby a teacher is "never in full possession of herself, her student, or of the texts she works with."[30]

I realize now that I also resisted the knowledge that a reader-response approach to texts created fear in me. Rather than claim my fear, I ignored it. Since this new approach displaced my usual position of authority (a position founded on the illusion that authority may be mastered), I found myself in an uncertain place where pedagogy did not unfold in a predictable way. In other words, I had constructed "pedagogy" as predictable, progressive, linear. I now see, through the implications of psychoanalysis for pedagogy, that pedagogy and a reader-response approach to texts do not advance in "linear progress, but through breakthroughs, leaps, discontinuities, regressions, and deferred action."[31]

The challenge of enacting a new stance toward texts brought with it a need for me to construct a new position of authority. However, I resisted this reconstruction. My need to maintain the authority I had enacted in the past, founded on "known" authorities, caused me to cite literary theory, Marxism and feminism, in my "spontaneous" lecture in the podium incident. Doing this left me feeling more comfortable, less vulnerable, but still without a way to enact an authority in this new approach to texts. I needed to work through the uncertainty a response approach to texts brought by seeing myself as one who guides the process of meaning-making. This then would be a paradoxical enactment of pedagogy as Ellsworth describes it—a paradox that occurs when readers become responsible for creating meanings from a text. This enactment of pedagogy requires "A teacher's taking control" in order "to manipulate students into taking responsibility" for the meanings they make—for the knowledge they construct."[32]

Thus, I still needed to guide Gina to an understanding of a different approach to texts, but encourage her to make her own meaning. Her resistance to this new approach to texts said that she wanted direction not only for the lesson, but from an authority. She desired certainty. Had I been able to offer the theoretical grounding she needed to then assume a response approach to texts, she may have been able to claim her own authoritative interpretation of *Equus*.

I now realize that my initial either/or framing of the Gina episode rested on two opposing constructs of text: either I opened textual interpretation to any comment, an over-determination of the reader, or I directed textual interpretation to knowledge of authorized interpretations, an over-determination of the text. Had I an appreciation for Rosenblatt's theory of reading as a transaction between the text *and* the reader during the Gina incident, I would have understood that "a sharp demarcation between objective and subjective becomes irrelevant, since they are, rather, aspects of the same transaction—a reader looks to the text, and a text is activated by the reader."[33] This view rejects a passive idea of reading and encourages the reader to be active in constructing meaning from experience. It says that during reading, both the text and the reader are modified.[34] If I had been able to offer Gina this theoretical guide through this process of reading, then I may have enhanced understandings of texts, interpretations and authority for both of us.

I now see that my either/or thinking and need for resolution is founded on what Phelan calls the "widespread belief in the possibility of full understanding and representation that reproduces the real exactly" that has committed us to "a concomitant narrative of betrayal, disappointment and rage."[35] Her insights are remarkable:

> EXPECTING UNDERSTANDING AND ALWAYS FAILING TO
> FEEL AND SEE IT, WE ACCUSE THE OTHER OF INADEQUACY,
> BLINDNESS, OF NEGLECT...
>
> MISUNDERSTANDING AS A POLITICAL AND PEDAGOGICAL
> TELOS CAN BE A DANGEROUS PROPOSITION, FOR IT INVITES
> THE BELLIGERENT REFUSAL TO LEARN OR MOVE AT ALL.
> THIS IS NOT WHAT I AM ARGUING FOR. *IT IS IN THE ATTEMPT
> TO WALK (AND LIVE) ON THE RACKETY BRIDGE BETWEEN
> SELF AND OTHER—AND NOT THE ATTEMPT TO ARRIVE AT ONE*

SIDE OR THE OTHER—THAT WE DISCOVER REAL HOPE. THE WALK IS OUR ALWAYS SUSPENDED PERFORMANCE—IN THE CLASSROOM, IN THE POLITICAL FIELD, IN RELATION TO ONE ANOTHER AND TO OURSELVES. THE INEVITABILITY OF OUR FAILURE TO REMAIN WALKING *ON* THE BRIDGE (WHEN THE STORMS COME WE KEEP RUSHING FOR THE DECEPTIVE "SAFETY" OF ONE SIDE OR ANOTHER) GUARANTEES ONLY THE NECESSITY OF HOPE.[36]

Looking back I realize that my desire to reside on one side of the bridge or the other was both a failure of pedagogy and a failure of authority. There is never arrival in a pedagogy; there is only a going. There is never a mastery of knowledge; there is only a continual stoking of a desire to know. Authority, like knowledge itself, requires a relationship, and like knowledge, it is not a "substance but a structural dynamic. . . not contained by any individual" but "irreducibly dialogic."[37] Thus, authority and knowledge must continually evolve within the pedagogical relationship. Authority must remain on that rackety bridge.

Now I also see, as did the medieval alchemist, that a failed process may bring with it new realizations and new understandings. My understanding is that ignorance and resistance are contained within the very construct of knowledge. Like the medieval alchemist, I need to recognize that things and their opposites may share common elements. This is the lesson of ignorance and knowing. I need to see, in other words, "that failure. . .can be productive."[38]

NOTES

1 Terry Eagleton, *Literary Theory: An Introduction* (Minneapolis: University of Minneapolis Press, 1983), 27.
2 Annie Dillard, *The Writing Life* (New York: Harper & Row, 1989), 73.
3 Eagleton, *Literary Theory: An Introduction*.
4 Peter Elbow, "What Do We Mean When We Talk about Voice in Texts?" in *Voices on Voice: Perspectives, Definitions, Inquiry*, ed. K Yancey (United States of America: National Council of Teachers of English, 1994).

5   Louise Rosenblatt, *Literature as Exploration*, Fourth edition (New York: The Modern Language Association of American, 1938/1983).
6   Peter J. Rabinowitz, "Whirl without End: Audience Oriented Criticism," in *Contemporary Literary Theory*, ed. G.D. Atkins and L. Morrow (Amherst: The University of Massachusetts Press, 1989).
7   Jeanne Connell, "Assessing the Influence of Dewey's Epistemology on Rosenblatt's Reader Response Theory," *Educational Theory* 46, no. 4 (1996): 400.
8   Robert Scholes, *The Rise and Fall of English: Reconstructing English as a Discipline* (New Haven: Yale University Press, 1998), 73.
9   Robert Usher and Richard Edwards, *Postmodernism and Education* (New York: Routledge, 1994), 127.
10 Derrida in Usher and Edwards, *Postmodernism and Education*, 127.
11 Eagleton, *Literary Theory*, 119.
12 Scholes, *The Rise and Fall of English*, 73.
13 Elizabeth Ellsworth, *Teaching Positions: Difference, Pedagogy, and the Power of Address* (New York: Teachers College Press, 1997), 14.
14 Paulo Freire, *Pedagogy of the Oppressed*, trans M.B. Ramos (New York: Herder and Herder, 1970).
15 Shoshana Felman, "Psychoanalysis in Education: Teaching the Terminable and Interminable," *Yale French Studies*, no. 63 (June 7, 1982): 28.
16 Lacan in Felman, "Psychoanalysis in Education."
17 Felman, "Psychoanalysis in Education."
18 Ibid., 26-29.
19 Felman, "Psychoanalysis in Education."
20 Lacan in Felman, "Psychoanalysis in Education," 28. Felman "reads through" Lacan, a disciple of Freud for the implications of psychoanalysis in pedagogy in the ensuing discussion.
21 Ibid., 29.
22 Ibid.
23 Ibid.
24 Ibid., 29-30.
25 Freud in Felman, "Psychoanalysis in Education," 30.
26 Felman, "Psychoanalysis in Education."
27 Lacan quoting Freud in Felman, "Psychoanalysis in Education," 30.
28 Felman, Psychoanalysis in Education," 31.
29 Felman, "Psychoanalysis in Education. "
30 Ellsworth, *Teaching Positions*, 163.
31 Felman, "Psychoanalysis in Education," 27.
32 Ellsworth, *Teaching Positions*, 150.
33 Rosenblatt, *Literature as Exploration*, 18.
34 Connell, "Accessing the Influence of Dewey's Epistemology."

35 Peggy Phelan, *Unmarked: The Politics of Performance* (New York: Routlege, 1993), 174.
36 Ibid.
37 Felman, "Psychoanalysis in Education," 33.
38 Ellsworth, *Teaching Positions*, 161.

Essay Seven

Pedagogy of Authority: A Matter of Meaning

"You must write and read as if your life depended on it," Rich says.[1] Imagine. Writing as if your life depended on it. She urges us "to write across the chalkboard, putting up there in public words you have dredged, sieved from your dreams, from behind the screen memories, out of silence—words you have dreaded and needed in order to know you exist."[2] Think back to all of the papers we've written. The notes. The letters. Perhaps these not proving we exist, but offering a kind of testimony that we do. (I'm reminded of Faulkner who said that all writing is an act intended to scratch "Kilroy was here" on the walls of the world.) But to write as if our lives depended on it?

I'm recalling now writings I've assigned over thirty years of teaching; the papers I've written. I still remember my senior research paper from St. Mary: The Elegy as a Literary Type Based on Milton's *Lycidas* and Tennyson's *In Memoriam*—topic assigned. (I remember, too, being told I wasn't "college material." Not personally told. Sr. Mercuri in addressing our class about standardized test scores said that anyone who fell below the 90th percentile (composite), shouldn't consider college. This in 1963.) But, I wonder, "Was there ever a time when I wrote with urgency, necessity, or sheer need?"

Once. This writing. I'm not sure if I always wrote at the top of my lungs or set loose all I needed to say, but I have written with a sense that something needed to be said. I've made a beginning. Annie Dillard insists, "one of the few things I know about writing is: spend it all, shoot it, lose it, all, right away, every time." She says the impulse to keep something to ourselves, something we've learned, is not only shameful but destructive. "Anything you do not give freely and abundantly becomes lost to you. You open your safe and find ashes." She adds this story: After Michelangelo died, someone found in his studio a piece of paper on which he had written a note to his apprentice. In the handwriting of his old age, he urges, "Draw, Antonio, draw, Antonio, draw and do not waste time."[3] I see what she means. I believe her and now, for the first time, I understand what it means to write from necessity. And now, for the first time, I call myself "author."

Beginning with a discussion of authoring and writing may seem tangential to these closing speculations about pedagogy of authority and how I go forth from here. Yet, they are quite germane. After all, I am the author of a pedagogy of authority. For another thing, authoring this text has been a self-conscious act of inquiry. All along I've made decisions to write with what Elbow calls a "recognizable or distinctive voice" and I have come to an "authoritative voice" as well.[4] These decisions were not merely a matter of style, although they were in keeping with the qualities of the essay as a genre and authoring from a feminist perspective.

I also see this "voicing" as an issue of interpretive research. By claiming voice in these ways, I underscore the point that I am not writing from some distanced or "objective" point of view. As Rich says, the writing is honest with "the sheer heft" of my living behind it.[5] Thus, the voice I speak with says that my experiences matter.

I also want to link the word author and pedagogy of authority by re-vising what it is to author. The history of the word author and authority are connected. "To author" once meant "a person who originates or gives existence to something, a begetter, *father*."[6] (For example, Gloucester in *King Lear* "authored" his illegitimate son, Edmund.) The idea that the writer "fathers" a text just as God fathered the world has been all-pervasive in Western literary civilization according to Gilbert and Gubar. If an author/father is owner of his text and of his reader's attention, he is also, owner/possessor of the subjects of his text, owner of those figures, scenes, and events—those brain children—he has incarnated in black and white and bound in cloth or leather. Thus, Giblert and Gubar say, because he is an *author*, a "man of letters," he, like his divine counterpart, is a father, master, ruler, and owner.[7]

Along with this notion of literary paternity, there has been the "historical confusion," according to Gilbert and Gubar, of literary authorship with patriarchal authority. Since male authors "father" texts and are in ownership of literary creations, and because an author defines characters in language and thus generates them, he owns them, controls them. Male authors, according to Gilbert and Gubar, use "fictional creations to talk back to other men" by generating alternative fictions. "From Eve, Minerva, Sophia and Galatea onward...patriarchal mythology defines women as created by, from, and for men, the children of male brains, ribs, and ingenuity." Thus, the "roots of authority tells us...that if a woman is man's property then he must have authored her, just as surely as they tell us that if he authored her she must be his property." In ending their discussion, these authors say that as a creation penned by man, woman has been penned up and penned in; she has been "sentenced, fated, framed, found guilty, found wanting" in his cosmologies.[8]

But my idea of author is neither father nor master. The former denies women and the later denies what I've come to know about understanding, knowledge, and reality. I no longer sit at the feet of this kind of author because he would deny the pen to my hand; he would assume the only valid knowing exists as something apart, outside of me. He would construct a fragmented story about the world and being. I seek to unify not master, to uncover the unconscious, reclaim my dreams. I seek to become *a part of the world, not apart from it*.

Neither is my idea of author singular. Through authoring this text on a pedagogy of authority, I now understand that the pedagogy I wish to enact is also authored, but not by one, not by someone who masters or pens anyone else in or locks them within language. (Even "masterpieces are not single and solitary births" says Virginia Woolf. "They are the outcome of many years of thinking in common, of thinking by the body of the people, so that the experience of the mass is behind the single voice."[9]) No, the pedagogy of authority I envision is like writing, not merely an individual act but a social one as well, happening within a context among teachers and students who come together to author meanings and their lives. Thus, a pedagogy of authority is co-authored by teacher and students, recognizes that they can shape the discourses of schooling and together transform them.

A pedagogy of authority invites students and teachers to take on with all seriousness the study of the ways discourses have shaped us and the way we shape discourses. It is aware that "A discourse author-ises certain people to speak and correspondingly silences others, or at least makes their voices less authoritative. A discourse is therefore exclusionary."[10] A pedagogy of authority aspires to understand and continually re-construct discourses so that no one is omitted. We are discursive in the way we author our texts, construct our knowledge, and the ways we relate to each other, even if our own understanding of these things is always partial and provisional.

To co-author pedagogy with students means that I need to guide them into taking responsibility for the texts we read and the knowledge we together produce. It means I act as a literary mentor who uses her experience to encourage multiple interpretations of texts, but who also keeps discussion from spinning into meaningless relativity. It means that I encourage each student "to take one's place in whatever discourse is essential to action and the right to have one's part matter."[11] What matters implies action not passivity, as Freire says, so that students will no longer be "docile listeners"[12] who wait for someone else to make meaning for them. It implies that students need to author their own understandings. It implies too, as Rich insists, that teachers take students seriously.[13]

I realize that co-authoring with students means I'll need to do a lot of talking, a lot of negotiating. It will require dialogue and reaching communal understandings. I suspect that I may even move back behind the podium on occasion. But I will be a different teacher when I am back there. I will remember what I wrote here and not be in that place for the first time.

I once felt that obedience to my will was more important than learning. But Milgram's study on *Obedience to Authority*[14] offers me chilling insight into ways that authority in unequal relationships may evoke trust and obedience in dangerous ways. Now I temper my authority. Since "the pedagogical relation itself is unpredictable, incorrigible, uncontrollable, unmanageable, disobedient,"[15] seeking obedient students may get only obedient students.

I know there will be resistances to a pedagogy of authority. Authoring a pedagogy or "oneself" and one's authority will not be easy. I know that I'll need to revise how I think about students and accept that things won't always move ahead smoothly: there will be resistances, and there need to be resistances. In fact, "There is nothing wrong with resistance if it can be led back to the knowledge of what it resists."[16] I agree with Ellsworth when she says that when students resist or don't want to see, when they don't "get it," we seldom think the problem is with understanding per se. "It's usually framed as a matter of some onerous relation between students and their broader social and cultural constraints," she says. "In other words, students would get it if only they had the right cultural competencies, intellectual skills, or moral virtues." But this way of thinking allows understanding to escape scrutiny, she says.[17] It denies the role of ignorance, resistance, and the unconscious in knowledge. I suspect that when the distance between reality and "self" closes, when the knower and known are no longer constructed as subject/object, when the distance between the conscious and unconscious lessens, then alienation, too, will diminish; unnamed resistance will lessen.

In thinking about a pedagogy of authority, I believe it's important to realize my past as much as possible. "I am a part of all that I have met," says an aged Ulysses as he reflects on his life. I, too, have come to see all things are a part of me. I've come to see that the people I've known and the places I've been have authored me too. They are the texts that I hold, sometimes consciously, sometimes in the unconscious. But I need to name them lest I speak *unknowingly* with their voices. In terms of literary texts and past traditions, I agree with Rich:

WE NEED TO KNOW THE WRITING OF THE PAST, AND KNOW IT DIFFERENTLY THAN WE HAVE EVER KNOWN IT; NOT TO PASS ON A TRADITION BUT TO BREAK ITS HOLD OVER US.[18] AS LONG AS WE CONTINUE TO MAKE NEW READINGS OF TRADITIONAL TEXTS AND NOT GIVE THEM AUTHORITY OVER US, THEY REMAIN UNFINISHED, WAITING FOR US TO CREATE NEW INTERPRETATIONS. THUS, IN A PEDAGOGY OF AUTHORITY, THE TEACHER OF LITERATURE "SUBSTITUTES AN APPEAL TO THE AUTHORITIES FOR THE MORE COMPLICATED PERFORMANCE OF A PUBLIC INTERPRETATION THAT CHALLENGES THE STUDENT TO DIALOGUE."[19]

Dialogue is not without its problems, I know, and this is not intended to say that all things become possible through dialogue, because it too can be used as a mask of domination. But, dialogue makes possible discursive understandings and gives way to meaning-making.

In the final analysis, this is how I construct pedagogy: as a discursive and meaning-making activity. This means that like any other text, pedagogy is continually shaped in the interpretation; it is never finished for it is always in the making. Like alchemy, a pedagogy of authority offers no recipe or formula to be handed down, copied, performed, packaged, or parceled out to others. Rather, as Berman claims, the practice of alchemy required a profound individual commitment, because each person had to break the divide between the conscious and the unconscious parts of the mind.[20] So, too, with a pedagogy of authority. It recognizes the unconscious and seeks to enclose rather than deny it. As Freire says, we need to make the distinction between possessing a consciousness rather than being conscious; we need to be *with* the world not merely be *in* the world.[21]

So even as I draw this essay to a close, place the last period at the end of the final sentence, I realize there really can be no ending. Authoring gives me the convention of ending, yet I know that this text will continue along in an un-finished way.

The text I am authorizing goes on because as I continue, I carry unwritten sentences and unwritten essays with me. Schubert says it well: Moreover, the essays that we each are write indelible essays on the world through the continuous flow of our being.²² It goes on because writing and reading within the interpretive tradition are never arrivals. I know, too, that there can be no "findings" or concrete conclusions to this text. There are only suggestions and implications that may give rise to other meanings, other texts, other authorings.

Notes

1 Adrienne Rich, "As if Your Life Depended on It," in *What is Found There: Notebooks on Poetry and Politics* (New York: W.W. Norton & Company, 1993)
2 Ibid., 33.
3 Annie Dillard, *The Writing Life* (New York: Harper & Row, 1989), 78-79.
4 Peter Elbow, "What Do We Mean When We Talk about Voice in Texts" in *Voices on Voice: Perspectives, Definitions, Inquiry*, ed. K. Yancey (United States of America: National Council of English Teachers, 1994).
5 Rich quoted in Elbow, "What Do We Mean When We Talk about Voice in Texts?" 32.
6 Edward Said, *Beginnings, Intention and Method* (New York: Basic Books, 1975).
7 Sandra Gilbert and Susan Gubar, *The Madwoman in the Attic: The Woman Writer and the Nineteenth-Century Literary Imagination* (New Haven, CT: Yale University Press, 1984).
8 Ibid., 12-13.
9 Virginia Woolf, *A Room of One's Own* (Orlando, FL: Harcourt Brace Jovanovich, 1957/1929), 65.
10 Robin Usher and Richard Edwards, *Postmodernism in Education* (New York: Routledge, 1994), 90.
11 Carolyn Heilbrun, *Writing a Woman's Life* (New York: Ballantine Books, 1988), 18.
12 Paulo Freire, *Pedagogy of the Oppressed*, trans. M.B. Ramos (New York: Herder and Herder, 1970).

13 Adrienne Rich, "Taking Women Students Seriously," in *On Lies, Secrets, and Silence: Selected Prose 1966-1978* (New York: W.W. Norton Company, 1979).
14 Stanley Milgram, *Obedience to Authority* (New York: Harper & Row, Publishers, 1969), 109.
15 Elizabeth Ellsworth, *Teaching Positions: Difference, Pedagogy and the Power of Address* (New York: Teachers College Press, 1997).
16 Patrick McGee, "Truth and Resistance: Teaching as a Form of Analysis," *College English* 49, no. 6 (1987).
17 Ellsworth, *Teaching Positions*, 46-67.
18 Adrienne Rich, "When We Dead Awaken: Writing as Re-Vision," in *On Lies, Secrets, and Silence: Selected Prose 1966-1978* (New York: W.W. Norton & Company, 1979), 35.
19 McGee, "Truth and Resistance," 677.
20 Morris Berman, *The Reenchantment of the World* (Ithaca, NY: Cornell University Press, 1981).
21 Freire, *Pedagogy of the Oppressed*, 62.
22 William Schubert, "Philosophical Inquiry: The Speculative Essay," in *Forms of Curriculum Inquiry*, ed., E.C. Short (Albany: State University of New York Press, 1991), 72.

BIBLIOGRAPHY

Arter, Judith, and Vicki Sandel. "Using Portfolios of Student Work in Instruction and Assessment." *Educational Measurement: Issues and Practices* (Spring 1992): 36-44.

Atkins, G. Douglas. "Introduction: Literary Theory, Critical Practice and the Classroom." In *Contemporary Literary Theory*. Edited by G.D. Atkins and L. Morrow. Amherst: The University of Massachusetts Press, 1989.

Berlin, James, and Robert Inkster. "Current-Traditional Rhetoric: Paradigm and Practice." *Freshman English News* (Winter 1980): 1-14.

Berman, Morris. *The Reenchantment of the World*. Ithaca: Cornell University Press, 1981.

Berthoff, Ann E. *The Making of Meaning: Metaphors, Models, and Maxims for Writing Teachers*. Upper Montclair, NJ: Boynton/Cook Publishers, Inc.

Biklen, Sari Knopp. "Foreword." In *Beginning in Retrospect: Writing and Reading a Teacher's Life*. Edited by P. Schmidt. New York: Teachers College Press.

Bloom, Leslie. *Under the Sign of Hope: Feminist Methodology and Narrative Interpretation*. Albany: State University of New York Press, 1996.

Blumenthal, Danielle. "Representing the Divided Self." *Qualitative Inquiry* 5, no. 3 (1999): 377-392.

Boorstin, Daniel. *The Discoverers*. New York, Vintage Books, 1983.

Bower, C.A. *The Promise of Theory: Education and the Politics of Cultural Change*. New York: Teachers College Press, 1987.

Brause, Rita S. "Foreword." In *Teaching College English and English Education: Reflective Stories*. Edited by T.H. McCracken, R.L. Larson and W.J. Entes. Urbana, IL: National Council of Teachers of English, 1998.

Britzman, Deborah P. "Cultural Myths in the Making of a Teacher: Biography and Social Structure in Teacher Education." *Harvard Educational Review* 56, no. 4 (November, 1986): 442-456.

Britzman, Deborah. "Institutional Biography," e-mail to author. (June 2000).

Britzman, Deborah. "Is There a Problem with Knowing Thyself? Toward a Poststructuralist View of Teacher Identity." In *Teachers Thinking, Teachers Knowing*. Edited by T. Shanahan. Urbana, IL: National Conference on Research in English, 1994.

Britzman, Deborah. *Practice Makes Practice: A Critical Study of Learning to Teach*. Albany: State University of New York Press, 1991.

Bruner, Jerome. *Acts of Meaning*. Cambridge, MA: Harvard University Press. 1990.

Bryk, Anthony S., Valerie E. Lee, and Peter B. Holland. *Catholic Schools and the Common Good*. Cambridge, MA: Harvard University Press, 1993.

Bullough, Robert V., and David K. Stokes. "Analyzing Personal Teaching Metaphors in Preservice Teacher Education as a Means for Encouraging Professional Development." *American Educational Research Journal* 31, no. 1 (1994): 197-224.

Burbules, Nicholas. "A Theory of Power in Education." *Educational Theory* 36, no 2 (1986): 95-114.

Butler, Judith. "Imitation and Gender Insubordination. In *Women, Knowledge, and Reality: Explorations in Feminist Philosophy*. Edited by A. Garry and M. Pearsall. New York: Routledge, 1996.

Campbell, Joseph with Bill Moyers. *The Power of Myth*. Edited by B.S. Flowers. New York: Anchor Books, Doubleday, 1988.

Ceroni, Kathleen M. "Biography of a Discipline." E-mail to author (July 2000).

Clark, Christopher M. "Asking the Right Questions about Teacher Preparation: Contributions of Research on Teacher Thinking." *Educational Researcher* 29, no. 2 (1988): 5-12.

Connell, Jeanne, "Assessing the Influence of Dewey's Epistemology on Rosenblatt's reader Response Theory." *Educational Theory* 46, no. 4 (1996): 395-413.

Connelly, Michael F. and D. Jean Clandinin. *Teachers as Curriculum Planners: Narratives of Experience*. New York: Teachers College Press, 1988.

Conway, Jill Kerr. *When Memory Speaks: Exploring the Art of Autobiography*. New York: Vintage Books, 1999.

Crawford, June, Susan Kippac, Jenny Onyx, Una Gault, and Pam Benton. *Emotion and Gender: Constructing Meaning from Memory*. London: Sage, 1992.

DeLauretis, Teresa. *Technologies of Gender: Essays on Theory, Film, and Fiction*. Indiana: Indiana University Press, 1987.

Dillard, Annie. *The Writing Life*. New York: Harper & Row, 1989.

Doll, Mary. "Beyond the Window: Dreams and Learning." *Journal of Curriculum Theorizing* 4, no. 1 (1982): 197-201.

Dooley, Deborah Anne. *Plain and Ordinary Things*. Albany: State University of New York Press, 1995.

Ellis, Carolyn. "Evocative Autoethnography: Writing Emotionally about our Lives." In *Representation and the Text: Re-framing the Narrative Voice*. Edited by W. Tierney and Y. Lincoln. Albany: State University of New York, 1997.

Ellsworth, Elizabeth. *Teaching Positions: Difference, Pedagogy, and the Power Address*. New York: Teachers College Press, 1997.

Emig, Janet. "Non-magical Thinking: Presenting Writing Developmentally in School." In *The Web of Meaning: Essays on Writing, Teaching, Learning, and Thinking*. Edited by D. Goswami and M. Butler. Upper Monclair, NJ: Boynton/Cook Publishers, Inc., 1983.

Felman, Shoshana. "Psychoanalysis and Education: Teaching the Terminable and Interminable." *Yale French Studies* no 63 (June 7, 1982): 21-44.

Ferguson, Ann. "Can I Choose Who I Am? And How Would That Empower Me? Gender, Race, Identities and the Self." In *Women, Knowledge, and Reality: Explorations in Feminist Philosophy*. Edited by A. Garry and M. Pearsall. New York: Routledge, 1996.

Finke, Laurie. "Knowledge as Bait: Feminism, Voice, and the Pedagogical Unconscious." *College English* 55, no. 1 (1991): 7-27.

Fiske, John. *Understanding Popular Culture*. London: Routledge, 1991.

Fleckenstein, Kristie. "Images, Words, and Narrative Epistemology." *College English* 58, no. 8 (1996): 914-933.

Freire, Paulo. *Pedagogy of the Oppressed*. Translated by Myra Bergman Ramos. New York: Herder and Herder, 1970.

Frost, Robert. "The Black Cottage." In *A Pocket Book of Robert Frost's Poems*. New York: Washington Square Press, 1964.

Gans, H.J. "The Participant-Observer as Human Being: Observations on the Personal Aspects of Field Work." *In Institutions and the Person: Papers Presented to Everett C. Hughes*. Edited by H.S. Becker, B. Geer, D. Riesman, and R.S Weiss. Chicago: Aldine, 1968.

Garman, Noreen. "The Study of Educational Myth and Clinical Supervisory Practice." Paper read at The American Educational Research Association in Montreal, Canada, 1983.

Garman, Noreen and Maria Piantanida. "The Academic/Professional Portfolio." *The Australian Administrator* 12, no. 3 (1991): 1-7.

Gilbert, Sandra, and Susan Gubar. *The Madwoman in the Attic: The Woman Writer and The Nineteenth-Century Literary Imagination*. New Haven: Yale University Press, 1984.

Gilligan, Carol. *In a Different Voice: Psychological Theory and Women's Development*. Cambridge, MA: Harvard University Press, 1982.

Greene, Maxine. "The Lived World." In *The Education Feminist Reader*. Edited by L. Stone. New York: Routledge, 1994.

Griffin, Susan. "Split Culture." In *The Schumacher Series*. Edited by S. Kumin. London: Blonde & Briggs, 1984.

Hairston, Maxine. "The Winds of Change: Thomas Kuhn and the Revolution in the Teaching of Writing." In *Landmark Essays on Writing Process*. Edited by S. Perl. Davis, CA: Hermagoras Press, 1994.

Hampl, Patricia. "Memory and Imagination." In *The Dolphin Reader*. Edited by D. Hunt. Boston: Houghton Mifflin Company, 1986.

Harris, Wendell. "Reflections on the Peculiar Status of the Personal Essay." *College English* 58, no. 8 (1996): 934-953.

Haug, Frigga. *Female Sexualization: A Collective of Memory*. Translated by Erica Carter. London: Verso, 1987.

Hazo, Sam. *The Pittsburgh that Starts within You*. Pittsburgh, PA: Byblos, 1986.

Hazo, Sam. Poetry Workshop Presentation of the International Poetry Forum, Pittsburgh, PA, 1999.

Heilbrun, Carolyn. *Writing a Woman's Life*. New York: Ballantine Books, 1988.

Heshusius, Lous and Keith Ballard. "How Do We Count the Ways We Know? Some Background to the Project." In *From Positivism to Interpretivism and Beyond: Tales of Transformation in Educational and Social Research (The Mind-Body Connection)*. Edited by L. Heshusium and K. Ballard. New York: Teachers College Press, 1996.

Hisrich, Sister Maria Thecia and Father John M. Unger. *A Sermon in Sculptured Stone and Jeweled Glass: Sacred Heart Church, Commemorative Volume*. Pittsburgh: Printed in the United States, 1976.

Jensen, Julie. "Broad Shoulders and Big Issues: Council Leaders Tell Their Stories." *English Journal* 89, no. 3 (2000): 97-103.

Johnston, Sue. "Images: A Way of Understanding the Practical Knowledge of Student Teachers." *Teaching & Teacher Education* 8, no. 2 (1992): 123-136.

Keen, Sam and Anne Valley-Fox. *Your Mythic Journey: Finding Meaning in Your Life through Writing and Story-Telling*. New York: Putnam Publishing, 1989.

Kermode, Frank. "Memory and Autobiography." *Raritan* 15, no. 1 (1995): 36-51.

Kilbourn, Brent. "Fictional Theses." *Educational Researcher* (December 1999): 27-32.

Korthagen, Fred A. and Joseph Kessels. "Linking Theory and Practice: Changing the Pedagogy of Teacher Education." *Educational Researcher* (May 1999): 4-17.

Laidlaw, Linda and Dennis Sumara. "Transforming Pedagogical Time." *Journal of Curriculum Theorizing* 16, no. 1 (2000): 9-23.

Langer, Susanne. "Speculations on the Origins of Speech and Its Communicative Function." In *Philosophical Sketches*. Baltimore: Johns Hopkins, 1962.

Lopate, Phillip. *The Art of the Personal Essay: An Anthology from the Classical Era to the Present*. New York: Anchor Books, 1994.

Luke, Carmen. "Feminist Pedagogy Theory: Reflections on Power and Authority." *Educational Theory* 46, no. 1 (1996): 283-302.

McEwan, Hunter. "The Functions of Narrative and Research on Teaching." *Teaching and Teacher Education* 13, no. 1 (1997): 85-92.

McGee, Patrick. "Truth and Resistance: Teaching as a Form of Analysis." *College English* 46, no. 6 (1987): 667-678.

McMahon, Patricia. "From Practice to Story to Research Text: The Role of Arts-based Research in Teacher Inquiry." Paper read at The American Educational Research Association in Montreal, Canada, April 22, 1999.

Milgram, Stanley. *Obedience to Authority*. New York: Harper & Row Publishers. 1969.

Miller, Janet. "What's Left in the Field: A Curriculum Memoir." Paper read at The American Educational Research Association in Montreal, Canada, April 22, 1999.

Oxford English Dictionary. *The Compact Edition of the Oxford English Dictionary*. Oxford: Oxford University Press, 1971.

Palmer, Parker J. *The Courage to Teach: Exploring the Inner Landscape of a Teacher's Life*. San Francisco: Jossey-Bass Publishers, 1998.

Perl, Sondra. "Understanding Composing." In *Landmark Essays on Writing Process*. Edited by S. Perl. Davis, CA: Hermagoras, 1980/1994.

Phelan, Peggy. *Unmarked: The Politics of Performance*. New York: Routledge, 1993.

Pinar, William and William Reynolds, Patrick Slattery, and Peter Taubman. *Understanding Curriculum: An Introduction to the Study of Historical and Contemporary Discourses*. New York: Peter Lang Publishing, Inc. 1995.

Polanyi, Michael. *Personal Knowledge: Towards a Post-critical Philosophy*. Chicago: University of Chicago Press, 1066.

Rabinowitz, Peter J. "Whirl without End: Audience-oriented Criticism." In *Contemporary Literary Theory*. Edited by G.D. Atkins and L Morrow. Amherst: The University of Massachusetts Press, 1989.

Recchio, Thomas. "On the Critical Necessity of 'Essaying'." In *Taking Stock: The Writing Process Movement in the 90's*. Edited by L. Tobin and T. Newkirk. Portsmouth, NH: Boynton/Cook Publishers, 1994.

Rich, Adrienne. "As If Your Life Depended on It." In *What is Found There: Notebooks on Poetry and Politics*. New York: W.W. Norton & Company, 1993.

Rich, Adrienne. "Claiming an Education." In *On Lies, Secrets, and Silence: Selected Prose 1966-1978*. New York: W.W. Norton & Company, 1979.

Rich, Adrienne. *On Lies, Secrets, and Silence: Selected Prose 1966-1978*. New York: W.W. Norton & Company, 1979.

Rich, Adrienne. "Taking Women Students Seriously." In *On Lies, Secrets, and Silence: Selected Prose 1966-1978*. New York: W.W. Norton & Company, 1979.

Rich, Adrienne. "When We Dead Awaken: Writing as Re-vision." In *On Lies, Secrets, and Silence: Selected Prose 1966-1978*. New York: W.W. Norton & Company, 1979.

Richardson, Laurel. "Writing: A Method of Inquiry." In *Handbook of Qualitative Research*. Edited by N.K. Denzin and Y.S. Lincoln. Thousand Oaks, CA: Sage, 1994.

Richardson Laurel. *Fields of Play: Constructing an Academic Life*. New Brunswick, NJ: Rutgers University Press, 1997.

Rosenblatt, Louise. *Literature as Exploration*. 4th Edition. New York: The Modern Language Association of America, 1938/1983.

Said, Edward. *Beginnings: Intention and Method.* New York: Basic Books, 1975.

Scholes, Robert. *The Rise and Fall of English: Reconstructing English as a Discipline.* New Haven: Yale University Press, 1998.

Schubert, William. "Philosophical Inquiry: The Speculative Essay." In *Forms of Curriculum Inquiry.* Edited by E.C. Short. Albany: State University of New York Press, 1991.

Schwandt, Thomas. "On Understanding Understanding." *Qualitative Inquiry* 5, no. 4 (1999): 451-654.

Shakespeare, William, "Hamlet, Prince of Denmark." In *The Complete Works of Shakespeare.* Edited by David Bevington. 3rd Edition. Glenview, IL: Scott, Foresman and Company, 1980/1599.

Shakespeare, William, "King Lear." In *The Complete Works of Shakespeare.* Edited by David Bevington. 3rd Edition. Glenview, IL: Scott, Foresman and Company, 1980/1599.

Smith, David. "Hermeneutic Inquiry: The Hermeneutic Imagination." In *Forms of Curriculum Inquiry.* Edited by E.C. Short. Albany: State University of New York Press, 1991.

Sommers, Nancy. "Between the Drafts." In *Women/Writing/Teaching.* Edited by J.Z. Schmidt. Albany: State University of New York Press, 1998.

Stafford, William. "A Way of Writing." In *Landmark Essays on Writing Process.* Edited by S. Perl. Davis, CA: Hermagoras Press, 1994.

Thompkins, Jane. *A Life in School: What the Teacher Learned.* New York: Addison-Wesley Publishing Company, Inc., 1996.

Thompkins, Jane. "Look Back in Anger." *Teachers Magazine.* (October 1996): 42-45.

Usher, Robin and Richard Edwards. *Postmodernism and Education.* New York: Routledge, 1994.

Walkerdine, Valerie. "Progressive Pedagogy and Political Struggle." In *Feminism and Critical Pedagogy*. Edited by C. Luke and J. Gore. New York: Routledge, 1992.

Waller, Willard. *The Sociology of Teaching*. New York: John Wiley & Sons, Inc., 1932.

Watt, E.D. *Authority*. New York: St. Martin's Press, 1982.

Weedon, Chris. *Feminist Practice and Poststructuralist Theory*. Oxford: Blackwell Publishers, 1987.

Welker, Robert. *The Teacher as Expert: A Theoretical and Historical Examination*. Albany: State University of New York Press, 1992.

Wharton, Edith. *Ethan Frome*. New York: Penguin Books, 1987.

Wilbur, Richard. "Advice to a Prophet." In *The Poems of Richard Wilbur*. New York: Harcourt Brace Jovanovich, Publishers, 1963.

Woolf, Virginia. *A Room of One's Own*. Orlando, FL: Harcourt Brace Jovanovich, 1957.

Young, Richard. "Paradigms and Problems: Needed Research in Rhetorical Invention." In *Research and Composing*. Edited by C. Cooper and L. Odell. Urbana, IL: National Council of English Teachers, 1978.

Learning Moments Press

Learning Moments Press is a small, independent publishing company dedicated to sharing the wisdom that comes from thoughtful reflection on experience. The Wisdom of Practice Series showcases the work of individuals who illuminate the complexities of practice as they strive to fulfill the purpose of their profession.

Cooligraphy artist Daniel Nie created the logo for Learning Moments Press by combining two symbol systems. Following the principles of ancient Asian symbolism, Daniel framed the logo with the initials of Learning Moments Press. Within this frame, he has replicated the Adinkra symbol for *Sankofa* as interpreted by graphic artists at the Documents and Designs Company. As explained by Wikipedia, Adinkra is a writing system of the Akan culture of west Africa. *Sankofa* symbolizes taking from the past what is good and bringing it into the present in order to make positive progress through the benevolent use of knowledge. Inherent in this philosophy is the belief that the past illuminates the present and that the search for knowledge is a life-long process.

www.ingramcontent.com/pod-product-compliance
Lightning Source LLC
Chambersburg PA
CBHW050541300426
44113CB00012B/2212